W9-AIU-996

Frenchmen,
Desire,
Good Children

Frenchmen, Desire, Good Children

. . . And Other Streets of New Orleans

in words and pictures by John Chase

PELICAN PUBLISHING COMPANY
GRETNA 2012

For Nick

Copyright © 1949, 1960, 1977, 1988
By John Churchill Chase

Published by Robert L. Crager & Co., 1949, 1960
Published by arrangement by Pelican Publishing Company, Inc., 2001
First Pelican edition, October 2001
Second printing, September 2004
Third printing, December 2007
Fourth printing, May 2010
Fifth printing, July 2012

The word "Pelican" and the depiction of a pelican are trademarks
of Pelican Publishing Company, Inc., and are registered
in the U.S. Patent and Trademark Office.

Library of Congress Card No.: 49-48566

No portion of this book may be reprinted in any form without
the written permission of the publisher, except by a reviewer who
wishes to quote brief passages for inclusion in a review for a
newspaper or magazine.

Designed by Marshall Lee

Printed in the United States of America
Published by Pelican Publishing Company, Inc.
1000 Burmaster, Gretna, LA 70053

CONTENTS

BUT FIRST —

DETOUR!

*O*NCE upon a time, while minding my own business drawing historical cartoons, I became intrigued with the realistic manner in which the street names of New Orleans told my city's lusty history.

One night in 1943 I gave a short talk on the subject before the Toastmasters Club. The subject, in turn, intrigued my listeners. From this beginning came requests for other talks until, in number, these lectures have been more than a hundred. I do not think, in the whole history of New Orleans, that anyone has ever spoken from the platform more about the same thing without being either elected or defeated for public office.

In the course of these lectures my information and source material was corrected and corrected again as the story of the names of the streets was exposed to more and more critical and well-informed audiences. Thus, accidentally, I found myself—a simple cartoonist—breathing down the necks of historians, daring to question and double check their holy writ.

Historians are skillful people, who reach over their shoulders and drag back the past by its heels. Then, as it lies prostrate in their presence, they relentlessly and intimately write all about it. In defense of historians, a subject such as the street names of New Orleans is not one that can be so recalled. Tangled property lines of by-gone days, and rusting iron pipe markers of methodical surveyors bind and pin the subject to ancient times and to modern times as well. In a city as old as New Orleans, the paths of the streets are indelible markings of yesterday, which the law of the land retains for today, and for the eternal tomorrows. How, indeed, can an historian consider the streets historical when they are in front of his house, and around all the corners? How can he drag back the past, when he parks his car in it?

And so I was left out on the streets. I discovered that, just as much as the quaint and crumbly buildings of the Vieux Carré, the crazy quilt pattern of New Orleans' streets, and the names given them by many namers have a story to tell. On the pages that follow is the story I found. I am afraid it is historical.

Many people, many sources provided the information which has gone into this story. I acknowledge the helpfulness of all who have published books about New Orleans; from Jean Penicaut, Iberville's carpenter who laid aside his hammer and saw to write the first on-the-scene account of this neighborhood, to the authors of the last edition of the City Directory. I deeply appreciate the cooperation and courtesy of Mr. John Hall Jacobs, director of the New Orleans Public Library; Mr. George King Logan, assistant director; Miss Ruth Reynaud, chief of reference; and all the staff. Similarly am I appreciative of the treatment accorded me at Tulane's library, where Dr. Garland Taylor is director, and Miss Marguerite D. Renshaw heads the fine reference department.

For maps, charts, surveys, and much other literal and graphic material I am indebted to the custodians of the Louisiana Museum and Library, the City Archives (a department of the Public Library), the Notarial Archives, and to the engineers of the Sewerage and Water Board and the City Engineer's office. Especially do I acknowledge the helpful personal interest of Mr. Errol Kelly, Mr. Horatio Gilbert, Mr. Marcel T. Ducros, Mr. Francis Burns, Rev. Edward F. Murphy, Mr. Stanley Clisby Arthur, Mr. Edgar A. Perilloux, Mr. Cecil Murphy, Mr. William B. Wisdom, Mrs. Benjamin W. Yancey, Mr. Malcolm Arnault, and Miss Essae M. Culver of the Louisiana Library Commission.

And lastly, now that it is finished, I gratefully acknowledge the influence of Miss Margaret Ruckert, City Archivist, who insisted that I write this book and that I finish it; of Dr. Lydia Frotscher, who insisted that the book be in English with paragraphs, commas, etc. etc.; and of my wife who was at all times my first critic and my first assistant, and who says that she does so believe that I was at the library all the times I said I was, and not at the Sazerac Bar. I also wish to thank the bartenders of the Sazerac Bar.

John Chase

New Orleans

Wilderness – and a Street

WILDERNESS —
AND A STREET

A ROAD is a way of intercommunication between two different places. A street is such a road with some degree of preparation or maintenance.

The Romans designated their fine highways as *strata,* because they had prepared them with *stratums,* or layers, of surfacing. The Latin *strata* became the Anglo-Saxon *straet,* and thence the English *street.* In the early cities of England all the roads were surfaced or paved, and came to be called streets.

So the name for a road in a city became street. In this accepted sense, it no longer matters whether it is surfaced or not. This is especially true of New Orleans, where it costs many times more than any other American city to pave and maintain a paved street. As late as 1949 only 580 of 1,148 miles of streets were paved.

In the city's early days, city blocks were called islands, and they were islands with little banks around them. Logically, the French called the footpaths on the banks, *banquettes;* and sidewalks are still so called in New Orleans.

The streets, however, were always called streets—or the French equivalent, *rue;* and the Spanish, *calle.*

But in its larger sense, a street is an established, maintained way of intercommunication for the means of transportation available. The Mississippi River in North America, when the first Europeans discovered it, became from the start what it has remained: an established route of continental intercommunication, or a street.

In the lower valley of this river, in the region where New Orleans was set, countless lesser streams (called by the Indians *bayuks,* and by the white men bayous), together with lakes and the great river itself, all formed a useful and well used system of intercommunication. To the Indians, the explorers, the voyageurs, and the intrepid coureurs de bois these were streets.

But when we think of a street, something more substantial comes to mind. Something dryer, even for New Orleans. Here in this wilderness there was such an established and maintained public way, an ancient overland portage between the river and one of the bayous. At its junction with the river Jean Baptiste Le Moyne, Sieur de Bienville, set his city of New Orleans. Bienville named the bayou, St. John, for his patron saint, but the street he gave no name.

Paradoxically, it has never been called a street, although it is now one in both definitions of the word. This portage, this established and maintained way of intercommunication, this dean of all New Orleans streets, older than them all and older than the city itself, is listed in the nomenclature—literally translated from the French—as Bayou Road!

4

De Soto, conquistodoro of Spain, discovered the Mississippi river in 1541. One hundred and thirty-two years later, starting from New France, or Canada, Marquette and Joliet descended the river to the mouth of the Arkansas. Nine years after that, in April of 1682, LaSalle floated an expedition down the Mississippi all the way to its mouth. There he raised a cross, unfurled the Lily Flag of Bourbon France, and claimed all the valley of the river for his king, Louis XIV. He named it Louisiane.*

(You learn all this in the fifth grade. However, in New Orleans today there is a De Soto street and a Spain street. There is also Canada street, France street, and streets named for Marquette, Joliet and LaSalle. There is a Louis XIV street in Lakeview, and a Bourbon street in the Vieux Carré.)

But Louis XIV wasn't much interested in this new land. He was more interested in Madame de Montespan. (You don't learn that in the fifth grade.)

In 1682 Louis was at the height of his power; the France he ruled was the most influential nation in Europe. His wife was Marie-Thérèse, Infanta of Spain; her half-brother was Charles II of the Hispanic kingdom, and he was without heir. Upon her marriage to Louis, she had renounced all claim to Charles' throne; nevertheless, Louis had always schemed that the next occupant of that royal perch should be a Bourbon. All that was needed was the death of his Spanish brother-in-law who was in poor health.

---

* The present name, Louisiana, is a curious mingling of the French, *Louisiane;* and the Spanish, *Luisiana.* Somewhat similarly, Mississippi stems from the Algonquin language, in whose tribal domain the river started. These Indians called it *miss* for "big," and *sipi* for "river." The Big River picked up the meaningless remainder of its name as it flowed southward.

5

So when LaSalle returned to France to tell of his accomplishment, it was into this atmosphere of court intrigue and shady politics that he entered when he was granted audience with his king.

One can picture Louis sitting there reading the latest report of the waning health of the Spanish king, as LaSalle breathlessly begins his great story. Enthusiastically he begs for ships, men, and provisions to begin a colonial empire for France in the New World. Louis' bored eyes stare at the map spread before him, still wondering why the pulse of Charles II isn't weaker than it was last week. His gaze comes to rest on Mexico. Mexico, the rich Spanish possession! Why, it is adjacent to the new territory which this LaSalle is jabbering about. Here is something!

So LaSalle is granted an expedition of four ships, with an admiral in command, to sail him back to Louisiana to establish a settlement. But not at the mouth of the Mississippi River. Such nonsense. Put the settlement as close to the border of Mexico as he could squeeze. What Louis XIV wanted was an advance base to raid golden Mexico when the time was ripe.

LaSalle set off on his last ill-fated journey to America. Stubbornly he was determined to place the settlement on the Mississippi—king or no king. But he was uncertain of the location of the river's mouth, and he never found it. The vessels sighted land far to the westward, actually closer to Mexico than the mouth of the Mississippi.

Here LaSalle left the ships, and set out overland to find the river. But he never did; he got lost. Then, desperately, he sought to lead his band northward to Canada, but he got lost again. At this point his exasperated men murdered him.

For ten years France did nothing more about Louisiana.

Then, in the closing years of the 17th century, Spain proclaimed to the world that all the territory bordering on the Gulf of Mexico was Spanish by reason of the original discoveries of Pinedo in 1519. The king of Spain was still in poor health, but he wasn't dead—neither was he asleep.

France and England disputed this ruling of Spain in her own favor. They contended that claim without occupation was not binding. All three nations hustled expeditions off to the Gulf Coast.

Pierre Le Moyne, Sieur de Iberville, a Canadian by birth and a distinguished officer of the French navy, headed the French party. He was an older brother of Bienville, who was one of his band. Like LaSalle before them, these two Le Moyne brothers were ambitious to carve an empire for France in the wilderness of Louisiana.

After a pause at Santo Domingo, where they learned no news of British or Spanish expeditions had been heard, Iberville sailed into the Gulf. He sighted land and found a party of Spaniards building a settlement to be named Pensacola. Santo Domingo's news sources were hardly reliable. Nevertheless, the stronger French fleet left the Spaniards unmolested, and continued westward along the coast.

After two days' sailing, an island was sighted which appeared to screen a large bay. A landing party put ashore found the island strewn with human bones. Iberville thought that a fitting name for the place would be Massacre Island, and he so wrote into his journal. The water behind this isle was Mobile Bay. After futile efforts to make contact with the timid Indians on the mainland, the squadron pushed westward.

Iberville's journal reports sighting other islands, and

the reasons for the names he gave them. Horn Island was
so called because a sailor dropped a horn overboard as the
vessels passed; the ships anchored at the second island, and
so it was named Ship Island. A highly imaginative lookout,
peering through his glass, sang out that another island
ahead was overrun with cats. So Cat Island got its name,
although the "cats" were raccoons, creatures unknown to
Europeans.

From the Ship Island base, small boats were dispatched
to investigate westward and northward. It was then that
the Chandeleurs were discovered and so named, because
it happened on the feast of Chandeleur, or Candlemas.
Meanwhile, another boat found Deer Island; and the snug
harbor behind it. At last a base for operations to locate
the Mississippi was acquired.

Efforts to make friends with the Indians then became
the first order of business. Any information about the location of the Mississippi would be helpful, but the Indians
were elusive. Finally an old man, too lame to run, was
caught. He was treated royally, and lavished with gifts. On

the beach in plain sight of savage eyes, which they knew were following their every move, the French built him a cozy shelter, and a roaring fire to warm him. Then they diplomatically withdrew, leaving this example of French generosity and friendly intentions for the Indians to inspect. Unfortunately, the roaring fire ignited the grass and burned the old man to a crisp.

The Indians withdrew another mile into the woods.

Negotiations were finally established after a squaw was captured, loaded with trinkets, shown every kindness, and then allowed to escape. The Indians were the Biloxis, and the bay was named for them.

One day Iberville returned from a scouting trip in the woods to find Bienville entertaining a hunting party of Indians who called themselves the Bayougoulas. Bienville early displayed his ability to get along with Indians, a quality which was to profit the colony much in the future. The Bayougoulas knew the white men, they had heard of LaSalle and Tonti, their village was on the Mississippi. It was a great stroke of luck. Would the Bayougoulas lead them there? No, the Bayougoulas wanted to finish their hunting. But afterwards they would, and a rendezvous was decided upon. The French would light a beacon—a large fire—at a designated spot four days later.

At the appointed time the fire was lit, but it got out of hand and burned down the woods for miles around. They never heard of the Indians again. Iberville's organization appears to have been expert in every department of the business of exploring, except the matter of fires.

So it was without Indian guides that the French sailed two small boats along the windward side of the Chandeleur Islands and found the mouth of the Mississippi; but they ascended the stream 200 miles before they were certain of their river.

Two things would prove whether this was the Mississippi. One, if the settlement of the Indian villages coincided with the journals of LaSalle, a copy of which Iberville had; and two, if a letter left by Tonti with the Bayougoulas could be found. These journals were the writings of two priests, Father Zenobe Membre, and Father Louis Hennepin. There were also some notes reputed to be Tonti's. Tonti was LaSalle's faithful lieutenant, who, after his chief's disappearance in the Louisiana wilderness, spent some time trying to find him. He later swore that the Tonti notes which Iberville had were neither his information nor his handwriting.

Altogether, the information contained in these journals testified more to the vivid imaginations of their writers than to any of the local geography. Iberville was finally able to determine that the river was the Mississippi, but he was never able to make the journals coincide with anything he found.

This region of the lower valley of the Mississippi was the ancient domain of the Choctaw Indians, once a proud and powerful tribe of the Muskogian clan of North America, a people whose tribal legends boasted that they came from a hole in the ground. Choctaw country ranged along both sides of the river from its mouth to about as far north as Natchez, all the area north of Lake Pontchartrain and most of the present state of Mississippi. Villages of the Choctaws include such familiar place names in Louisiana and Mississippi (and such street names in New Orleans) as: Houma, Tangipahoa, Colapissa, Bayougoulas, Pascagoula, Avoyel, Taensas, Chinchuba, Pontchatoula, and perhaps Tchoupitoulas. But regardless of their origin, and whether they came from a hole in the ground as their legends claimed, as a nation of Indians these of the lower valley were in an advanced stage of racial suicide when LaSalle and Tonti, and later the Le Moyne brothers, intruded upon their heathen privacy. Small pox and plagues frequently wiped out whole villages; their astounding immorality and promiscuity, their neglect of children that amounted to wholesale infanticide, and the never-ending brawls between villages—called wars—all characterized a people who were well on their way to what is commonly termed the bow-wows.

Although the nature of their country required the Choctaws to lead a more or less amphibious way of life, they never learned to swim. In fact, they never learned to wash; they were a dirty and vermin-ridden crowd. Their outstanding characteristic was laziness; in truth it is doubtful that the world ever knew a class of people of whom it can more correctly be said that they didn't give a damn.

The men went naked ("without seeming to perceive it," the embarrassed French report) and the women wore girdles of tree bark around their middles. Younger women painted their teeth black, tattooed their faces and breasts, and wore numerous bracelets and bangles. This goes to prove that younger women are fussy even among a nation of people who don't give a damn.

Whereas the traditional Indian warriors wore feathers in their hair, the Choctaw braves wore feathers around their waists, sticking out behind like tails. This matter of the location of feathers is strikingly symbolic of the degree to which the Choctaws had slipped among Indians. Villages usually consisted of many more men than women;

there were no families, they were all just one family—or maybe it should be called a kennel.*

Sometimes Iberville and Bienville were able to pry a few lazy braves away from doing nothing and get them to guide the expedition. But when another village was

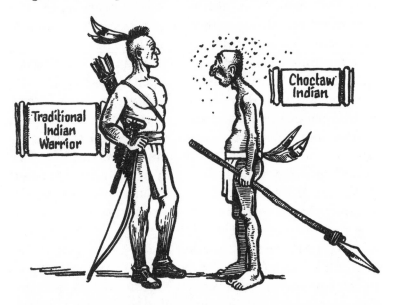

reached, these wolfish redskins began fraternizing with Choctaws of the opposite sex, refusing to leave. Grace King reports one instance of this that so angered Bienville that he furiously marched eighteen miles off into the woods. This is supposed to have amazed and frightened the Choctaw guides so much that they returned to their guiding chores. Miss King does not explain why this hike proved so successful; and it can only be deduced that the shock

* "Nothing is more difficult than the conversion of these savages . . . We must first make men of them, and afterwards work to make them Christians."—Father Gabriel Marest, Jesuit missionary in Louisiana in 1712.

12

of seeing a man walk eighteen miles, which was so remote from these lazy Indians' way of life, that their resolutions melted away—even their romantic resolutions.

As the expedition labored upstream, it encountered a spot where—the Indians declared—an overland portage led to a small bayou, which emptied into a lake called the Okwata. And by the Okwata, the Indians explained, they could return to their ships at Biloxi. This interested Iberville. Especially it interested Bienville, who would one day establish a city here.

A few days further upstream, another entry into the Okwata was pointed out by the guides. This was a pass— or manchac, as the Indians termed it—by which boats could easily enter the Okwata. Iberville resolved to return to the ships by this route, when he became convinced that he had located the Mississippi River; and he signaled the expedition to push on.

After more tortuous miles, the weary Frenchmen were shown a narrow passage. If the boats could be forced through, said the Choctaws from their comfortable seats in the sterns, a day's paddling and poling would be saved. Iberville gave orders to try it, and after hours of toil the boats squeezed through the cut-off. The French named this Cut Point—or, as it is still called, Pointe Coupee. In time, Old Man River himself, widened the cut point and adopted it for his regular passage. The river bed which he forsook has come to be known as False River.

Not far beyond Pointe Coupee, Iberville became convinced that he had found his river. The expedition turned about, and floated downstream to the place where the pass, or manchac, led to the Okwata. Iberville named this pass the Iberville River, and he also named the two lakes to which the river led. He called the larger one Pontchartrain, in honor of the Minister of Marine in France; the smaller one he named Maurepas, who was Pontchartrain's son.

Pontchartrain—if we believe the diarist, Saint Simon— was one of the most willful men who ever lived. Although Minister of Marine he hated admirals; especially he hated an admiral called the Comte Toulouse, who was a bastard son of the king. Unable to break Toulouse and deprive him of a command, he actually ruined the French navy so that nothing would remain for Toulouse to be an admiral of. Wide Lake Pontchartrain is the body of water directly north of the present city of New Orleans; there is also a Pontchartrain boulevard in the city, and a Maurepas street. But no street is called by the lake's former name, Okwata —a pretty Choctaw word which means wide water.

Iberville, back at his ship anchorage in Biloxi Bay, made ready to return to France, and obtain the essentials for a major settlement. It was, however, necessary to establish settlements near the ships until a master plan of colonization could be put into operation. So a fort was built at Biloxi, and another at Mobile. The name of Massacre Island was changed to Dauphin Island, after the heir of Louis XIV.

Soon after Iberville left for France, Bienville returned through Lake Pontchartrain for further explorations of the region of the Mississippi. He was particularly attracted to the neighborhood of the portage, and he headed up the small bayou, which received its name at this time—Bayou St. John. Where the portage met the river, he considered the best place for a settlement, and this eighteen year old youth persisted in this determination until the age of thirty-seven when he was destined to establish it.

Another incident at this time is notable, both as a revelation of the resourcefulness of Bienville, his audacity, and the origin of one of the more picturesque place names in the New Orleans neighborhood. It also reveals a Protestant Frenchman, who stands out as the most optimistic white man of his time in North America.

One day, cruising a few miles downriver from the portage and accompanied by six Canadians, Bienville came upon an English corvette! It was in truth one of several vessels sent out to seek settlement in the Mississippi country. But the expedition had spent the winter in Carolina. It was spring now, more comfortable for the English. Captain Banks, in command, had a boatload of settlers looking for a beachhead to set up an English colony. It developed that Bienville knew Captain Banks, the latter had once been a prisoner-of-war of Iberville after some unpleasantness in the far-away Hudson Bay country. Bienville explained to Banks that the French were busily building settlements upstream, and that French claim to the Mississippi valley was fully secured and binding by reason of these settlements. While on shipboard Bienville was approached by Monsieur Second, a Frenchman exiled from France because of his Protestant faith. He wanted to join one of these French settlements that Bienville spoke of springing up everywhere. Bienville agreed to this, but would Monsieur Second come back later? It would be better when the colonies were a little, more, er, firmly established. Second thereupon gave Bienville his address, both in Carolina and London; would Bienville please write him when everything was ready? Again Bienville agreed.

The next morning the English turned around, and Bienville saw to it that they passed out of the river before he returned to Biloxi by way of the portage. The point in the river where Captain Banks gave the command to about face is to this day called "English Turn."

Now, as for Monsieur Second—one wonders how long he waited for Bienville's letter, either at his Carolina address or London. For among Bienville's outstanding characteristics was an aversion to writing letters, reports, or anything else. The earlier days of New Orleans would be less obscure had Bienville been slightly more literary. It seems as if every time that boy had to write something, it was an excuse for another exploring trip. The inferences are that his favorite form of communication, next to oral, were smoke signals.

It is only a conjecture, therefore, that the first time Bienville visited the portage, the Houmas were not there; and that during the seventeen-year interval, before the first houses of New Orleans were raised, they came. They were there then, and for many years afterwards, the continuation of North Lopez street was called Encampment street, in recollection of the fact that these Indians maintained temporary quarters there at the headwaters of Bayou St. John. It accounts for a persistent historical recording that "the city was built near the site of a small Indian village called Tchou-Tchouma."

(It is also evident that the first workmen, sent to clear the site for the city, camped in this neighborhood of present-day Esplanade and Bayou St. John. Thus was further reason for a street in the neighborhood to be named Encampment.)

LaSalle, when he first met the Houmas on the Mississippi at its junction with the Red River, called them the

"Chouchouma Indians." A red stick (Baton Rouge) on the river bank separated the hunting ground of the Houmas from that of the Bayougoulas downstream. It is known that soon after LaSalle's passage, the Houmas gave sanctuary to the Taensas who had been run out of their neck of the woods by some war-whooping Chickasaws. No sooner had the Houmas let the Taensas in, when the latter attacked the Houmas and killed half of them. The remaining Houmas left, migrating eastward, during which migration they are said to have destroyed the Tangipahoas, just as the Taensas had half destroyed them. Lovely Indians, these Choctaws. This eastward migration ended at the Bayou St. John portage.

The Houmas are properly called Chakchiuma, or in Choctaw, Saktce-Homa, which means red crawfish. A crawfish was their tribal emblem. It is evident that had the Houmas not already intended moving from the portage, they would have once they learned how their name was being spelled and pronounced by the French. They ended up about fifty miles southwest of New Orleans, where the town of Houma now is.

Iberville returned from France with provisions and promises, but the latter were badly kept by the government of Louis XIV. Iberville died a few years later, and for six or seven years the colony and the colonists who peopled the tiny settlements of Mobile and Biloxi were virtually abandoned. A procession of governors was sent out, each of whom appeared to exceed the other in inefficiency and lack of what it takes to run a colony. To Bienville, who remained all the time, they were more trouble than the Indians.

In 1712, Antoine Crozat—called the richest man in Paris

—was granted a fifteen-year charter to operate Louisiana. Crozat's scheme was to build up settlements to trade with the Spaniards. Because he sought to make the colony a financial success without raising a hand to make it self-supporting, Crozat's scheme was doomed to failure. It wasn't helped by the sort of men he sent out to administer its affairs either. Probably the most astonishing among these was M. de la Motte Cadillac, whose principal contribution to Louisiana history appears to have been the reporting of Bienville, Major Boisbriant, Captain Chateaguay, and Lieutenant Serigny for failure to make their Easter duties.

It is regrettable that Bienville didn't keep a journal. One longs to know his thoughts and dreams as he pushed his pirogue through the bayous of the New Orleans neighborhood, and what he and his Canadian companions had to say about the men in France upon whom they must depend for everything, and who knew so little of their problems and cared even less. What they had to say about the governors sent out to them we would never know in any event, because these remarks would be unprintable.

That New Orleans became the first important place of human habitation in the lower valley, is due entirely to Bienville's persistence. The city owes its name to the politics of John Law and that Scotchman would never have had his General Bank and Company of the West were it not for the long misrule of King Louis XIV. Soon the street in the wilderness would have a city built upon it; a city which would become the capital of Louisiana. And, oh yes, one other thing happened to bring this about.

A French sergeant in the first capital of Louisiana fell asleep with his pipe in his mouth and burned down Biloxi.

Prelude to
a City

PRELUDE TO

A CITY

*E*IGHTY hopeless exiles laboriously clear away the thick growth of willows and palmettos, and hack at the tough cypress trees. They have been banished to this Louisiana wilderness for bootlegging salt to Frenchmen eager to escape the hated royal tax on that essential condiment—a nefarious levy, too, for it was twelve times more than the value of the substance taxed. In charge of the work gang is Bienville's trusted deputy, Jacques Barbazon de Pailloux. The clearing is for a town on the Mississippi River. Bienville has said it! He has received word from France! The time is 1718!

Like the Indian tribe whose wild domain this was, the European government, by whose authority these city-makers sweated, was crumbling with decay. It was as though the proud Choctaw Nation, and the swaggering House of Bourbon-Orleans—neither of whom knew of the other's existence—must both wither as they provide a beginning and give life to another in the society of cities.

In all the 128 years that the Bourbons ruled, the reign of

Louis XIV is notable. After seventy-two years it had just ended. Not only was it the longest; but, in plotting the grandeur of the House, Louis XIV's reign forms both sides of a triangle:—the tip-top upward sweep of the dynasty, its pinnacle of greatness, and its plunge downward—culminating with the clump of the guillotine's glistening blade on the back of the neck of Louis XVI. Seventy-five years after the establishment of New Orleans this would happen.

Although the first Bourbon to rule was Henry IV, the ancestor of the House is reputed to be one Peter, whose brother Jacques perpetuated the blood line.

There is a St. Peter street in the Vieux Carré.

But with well-sharpened pencils, the Bourbons can draw lineal connections back to a sixth son of the saint king, Louis IX. This was Robert, Count of Clermont. All the Bourbon kings who followed after Henry IV were christened Louis, but any other similarity with sainthood ends there.

The Vieux Carré includes a St. Louis street, and the first name of St. Philip street was Clermont.

The noble families of Conti, Condé, Vendome and Chartres also trace themselves back to these same beginnings, making them all kissing cousins to the Bourbons and Orleans.

Conti, Condé, Chartres, Bourbon, and Orleans were among the city's first streets. Vendome was an earlier name for Dauphiné, and until 1865, that section of Chartres from Jackson Square to Esplanade was Condé street.

The Orleans duchy of the Bourbon-Orleans axis became part of the royal domain in 1498. Louis XIV revived the title in favor of his brother, Philip, as had his father before him for his brother, Gaston. Just as Louis was a favored baptismal name for Bourbons, Philip was for the House of Orleans—and there is a St. Philip street in the Vieux Carré.

When Louis XIII died, leaving a five year old heir, the widowed Queen Ann and Cardinal Mazarin had practically to sit on Uncle Gaston to discourage him from proclaiming himself king. Today in all New Orleans no street is named Gaston. That five year old heir was Louis XIV. The beginning of the city of New Orleans must be prefaced with the story of this self-conscious, unmoral, arrogant, henpecked prince, whose rule also marks the beginning of the end of the Bourbons.

In fairness to him, it must be said that his parents gave him little besides life and a throne upon which to live it. His father, whom he never knew, took six weeks to make up his mind to die. Even at death's door, this confused, hesitant man was true to a lifelong characteristic. During his reign, Cardinal Richelieu made the decisions, and did the ruling. The France that Louis XIV inherited was of Richelieu's building. But perhaps his father's most conspicuous instance of hesitation was the matter of his heir, for Louix XIV was not born for twenty-two years after he and Ann of Austria walked down the center aisle of Notre Dame. The French people could never understand this.

Until Louis came of age, Queen Mother Ann and Cardinal Mazarin headed the Regency, and continued to dominate the government until the death of Ann, who survived the cardinal by four years. Neglected Louis grew to hate them both, mostly because they delayed their funerals so long; for this weakling prince did not become king in more than name until he was twenty-three. However, at this time his affairs with women considerably exceeded his years in number.

It is said no servant maid was secure from Louis' passing fancy. His love affairs began with the Macini sisters. First came the voluptuous Olympe, but this was a fleeting passion. It appears that Olympe was able to outrun him. Sister Marie Macini was less trouble. She was also less voluptuous but she didn't run, and for some time she was Louis' girl.

"But.... Olympe..."

Among these passion preliminaries was also the one-eyed Countess of Beauvais. Louis approached her on the blind side, and she is reported to have been his mistress— probably until she got a look at him with her good eye. Louis was never a very handsome prince.

The next object of Louis' affection was Henrietta, wife of his petticoat-loving brother Philip, Duke of Orleans. Effeminate Philip loved to wear petticoats! He was something of a problem around the palace for years; one never knew from day to day whether the Duke would be a Duke or a Duchess.* When the Queen Mother learned of this infatuation, she became fearful of incest. This is about the only thing in the morals line that ever disturbed the Bourbons. The Queen reasoned that the easiest way to get a boy's mind off of a girl was to get it on another girl. So she rushed one of Henrietta's ladies-in-waiting into Louis' waiting arms. This armful—Louise de la Baume Le Blanc, Duchesse de La Vallière—became the king's first mistress of any consequence. The consequences were a daughter who later married the Prince of Conti, and this is further reason for a Conti street in New Orleans.

At this point it becomes evident that—not counting servant maids—even in his affairs of the heart, Louis was having his mind made up for him by somebody else. His lone wolfing had netted him, (1) failure in the wake of the fleet-footed Olympe, (2) Marie, whom nobody else wanted to make love to, and (3) only a one-sided success in the case of the one-eyed Countess of Beauvais. His campaign for Henrietta was taken over by the Queen Mother, and the objective altered to La Vallière. In the case of his next mistress, the mistress was the master of the situation from the beginning.

François-Athénaïs de Rochechouart, Marquise de Montespan, was a skillful courtesan, ambitious, and also voluptuous. (Without that last qualification, the other two would have gone for nought in her business.) The Queen Mother was dead now. Louis was truly ruler, and de Montespan set her cap for him because of the power of the

* Many finical historians, disturbed that in its French spelling New Orleans is a masculine proper noun preceded by a feminine adjective, overlook this first Philip of Orleans. Although the city is named for the second Philip, he was preceded by this one of the jittery gender.

position of mistress to the king. She, too, had been a lady-in-waiting at the court.

A careful study of Louis' life reveals that he should have been insured against ladies-in-waiting, so many of whom appear to have been ladies-in-ambush for him. de Montespan became chummy with La Vallière to get within range of the king, and it wasn't long before former Lady-in-waiting La Vallière was what is best described as a lady-in-waiting for a streetcar. de Montespan moved in!

For twenty-four years this remarkable woman was mistress of the king of France. Louis ruled the most powerful and influential kingdom in Europe, and de Montespan ruled Louis. She bore him seven children, and so domineering and subtle was her influence over the king that his affection for this royal brood of bastards exceeded his fatherly love for his children born in wedlock. But retribution would come, and as the sins of the father returned to be visited upon the children, the father in lingering old age would share the anguish.

His favorite was his first born bastard, Louis-Auguste, who was titled the Duke du Maine. Gus inherited his mother's driving ambition, and his father's arrogance. But because he was neither voluptuous nor king along with those qualifications, he remained simply a royal bastard in every conceivable meaning of the term.

His younger brother was Louis-Alexandre, in whose favor the king revived the title of Comte de Toulouse. He appears to have been an exceedingly creditable character, and a capable officer of the French navy. Whereas du Maine excites contempt for his conduct, Toulouse earns consideration and pity for his perplexing station in life.

Besides these two princes, two daughters survived childhood. One Louis married to the Duke of Chartres, his brother's son; the other was equally well married to the Duke of Bourbon, son of the powerful Prince of Condé. du Maine also married one of Condé's daughters.

Visitors to New Orleans' Vieux Carré will recall that there the street nomenclature includes Dumaine, Toulouse, Bourbon, and also Chartres—a section of which was first called Condé.

While Louis' illegitimate children were young, a Madame Scarron was engaged as lady-in-waiting for them. She was later titled de Maintenon. This lady-in-waiting—you guessed it—eventually replaced de Montespan as the king's mistress. But de Maintenon was a girl who played for keeps, and ended her days as Louis' second wife.

There was a first wife, of course. Like all of Louis' women, his queen was selected for him by somebody else. His marriage with Marie-Thérèse, Infanta of Spain, appears to have been part of the Treaty of the Pyrenees. It also appears from this that if Spain lost the treaty, certainly Marie-Thérèse won little. She had nothing in common with the king except six children, and seems to have spent most of her time dodging her husband's mistresses in the corridors of the palace.

Like his father before him, Louis was blessed with a capable minister. His Colbert was an ingenious administrator. In ten years he doubled France's revenue. So Louis doubled his expenditures. Fifty years of extravagant wars which he fought to appease his vanity and thrill his women were matched by equally expensive periods of peace during which he built his fabulous palaces. Versailles is reputed to have cost two full years of French revenue, but Madame de Montespan thought it was adorable.

Colbert recommended bankruptcy, and died.

The king's last five years were sorrowful ones. In 1711 his son and heir, the Dauphin, died. The Duke of Burgundy, son of the Dauphin, inherited the title and became heir—and then died. Frenchmen became suspicious. A few days later when Burgundy's wife also died, they began to suspect that somebody was leaving poison around where heirs could get it. Then Burgundy's oldest son died, and the people began throwing rocks at the Duke of Orleans.

This depopulation of Bourbons left only Burgundy's second son—a suckling babe—as heir to the throne of Louis XIV. The king ordered a company of musketeers into the nursery. The babe lived to become Louis XV. Some observers of the life of Louis XV consider this a waste of musketeers.

The Duke of Orleans, who was openly accused of removing heirs one by one. was the king's nephew and son-in-law. Formerly the Duke of Chartres, he had succeeded to the Orleans title upon the death of Louis' petticoat-loving brother. Had this last babe died, his daughter would have become Queen for she was married to the Duke de Berry, third son of the Dauphin. Both Orleans and his daughter were fully capable of murder, but in spite of du Maine's loud accusations, their implication could never be proven. du Maine hated Orleans; for one thing a job of Regent was shaping up which du Maine coveted.

In May of 1715, the king disconcerted every peer in the realm by publishing a declaration that proclaimed du Maine and Toulouse to be precisely on the same footing as princes of the royal blood, and with all rights of succession to the throne. It was now Orleans' turn to hate and fear du Maine. However, in his will Louis named the Duke of Orleans Regent—but not with absolute power. du Maine and Toulouse were included on the board of Regency, along with other peers angry and jealous of the high places to which the old king had elevated his bastards. Such was the muddle and confusion Louis XIV left when he died September 8, 1716. The people rejoiced, and many got drunk.

Undeniably, the Age of Louis XIV was a great period in French history. But, as one historian puts it, the age was an exquisite, shining veneer. Like the violin whose veneer and polish give it tone and quality, the Age of Louis XIV had tone and quality. But beneath the glittering brilliant shell was rotting wood; the music could not long continue.

Today in modern New Orleans, streets such as Fontainebleau and Vincennes and Versailles recall the elegance of Louis XIV. But actually the city owes its beginning to the cancerous inside of the period, the rotting wood, and the efforts of the government which followed Louis to save something from the chaos. A government which subscribed to the bizarre financial system of John Law for reconversion—a government and system by whose orders 80 salt bootleggers, with de Pailloux in charge, were clearing a site for a town in Louisiana. Today, no New Orleans street honors Jacques Barbazon de Pailloux—certainly the first vested authority in the New Orleans area.

"...and Call It New Orleans"

"...AND CALL IT
NEW ORLEANS"

*T*HE kindest treatment that can be accorded Philip II,
Duke of Orleans and Regent during the infancy of Louis
XV, is to say the least about him. In an age notorious for
lax morals, in a Paris that boasted of more mistresses than
wives, at a court unmatched for licentious conduct,—
against this background, Philip stood out as one who led a
scandalous life. Openly accused of every crime and sin and
misconduct,—from the most venial breech, to murder and
unnatural relations with his degenerate daughter,—this
royal debauchee worked hard to be deserving of it all. And
yet, withal, he was a man of real if impotent abilities.

Perhaps his mother best explains his utter inability to
follow through, and the conspicuous lack of intestinal for-
titude which characterized her son's public life. In her
"Correspondence," the Duchess whimsically relates how
six fairies were invited to Philip's christening, and there
they endowed him with every gift and grace. But somehow
a seventh fairy was overlooked and not invited. Whereupon this Fairy No. 7 took cognizance of what Fairies Nos.

1 to 6 had bestowed upon Philip, and impishly added the proviso that none of it would ever be of any use to him. The seven years of his regency are a blank and fruitless interlude in French history.

Orleans termed his regency a reform movement. He restored Parliament which Louis XIV had abolished. Parliament, in return, set aside the old king's will, authorizing Orleans to rule with absolute power.

Thus, consistent with this movement, Orleans was able to reform du Maine back to a simple peer and royal bastard. He was purged from his lofty perch as prince of the blood, and so was Toulouse. But the amiable Toulouse, by another decree from Orleans, was restored to his previous position for the duration of his lifetime. du Maine's hatred for Orleans deepened. He and his wife headed a vicious minority at court in opposition to the regency.

One matter the Duke of Orleans could not reform or restore, even with all the power and majesty of an absolute monarch. The annual deficit was 65,000,000 francs. Louis XIV was one who gave the lie to the quip that "you can't take it with you." That old boy not only left nothing, but sixty-five million times less than nothing.

The Duke of Saint Simon suggested bankruptcy. A Scotchman named John Law recommended a mysterious financial system. The Regent with a fondness for novelty and mystery chose Law's plan, and permitted establishment of his General Bank.

As a Scotchman, John Law was the antithesis of what every Scotchman is supposed to be. Instead of hoarding money, he advocated spending it, and giving lots of it to everybody to spend! Law is called a lot of things; the inventor of inflation, the inventor of credit, an adventurer, a gambler, a man of genius. In parts, he was all of these—and also he was a kindred spirit of Philip, Duke of Orleans. He loved the ladies. (Plural, that is.)

His most severe critic declares "never did man possess in so perfect a decree the power of calculating and combining." Forced to flee from England after a duel over a woman, he learned of banking based on credit and "inside information" in Holland. Much of it he learned from the wives of bankers. He was a consistently successful gambler, because of his amazing powers of concentration and calculation. Gambling was his livelihood for fifteen years on the continent, during which interval he developed a system. A financial system for a nation. Preferably an absolute monarchy. After every prince in Europe had turned him down, the Duke of Orleans signed on the dotted line for France. John Law's operations began May 2, 1716—and this was also the cue for the beginning of New Orleans.

One writer, who was a contemporary of Law (and he sounds like one who had invested with him) explains the Scotchman's mysterious system as follows: ". . . he reasoned that a sovereign should pay his debts, not by encroaching upon his personal luxuries, but by attracting to himself all the gold and silver of his subjects. His scheme included making this so attractive to the subjects that they would rush to do this voluntarily. They should come to consider it a favor and a privilege—then, when they woke up and realized what they had done, they should not be able to blame anybody but themselves. The plan called for the establishment of a bank, the real capital of which would be the revenue of the state, and the accruing capital some unknown kind of commerce. Benefits from this commerce were calculated to keep pace with the imaginations of the investors in its increase. It would thus spur them on to partake of shares (in the enterprise) which were to be made in successive issues, and in proportion to the eagerness of the investors."

But in the beginning of his operations it does not appear that Law was so much of a scoundrel. Disaster resulted more from the meddling and greed of the Regent, than from the faults in Law's system. Law sought the concentration of the specie of the nation in a central bank, and for the conduct of business and affairs by letters of credit, called bank-notes. This bank, continually renewed and replenished by the revenues of the nation, would be authorized to issue its paper money, representing in part the gold and silver held on deposit. The people would be educated into accepting this paper in lieu of the hard specie. He succeeded in this and the initial success of his enterprise was enthusiastic.

To bolster faith in his operations, princes of the blood and influential peers were given first choice to buy stock in the bank, and in the company organized in conjunction with the bank. Thus let in on the ground floor, they reaped early dividends and the enthusiasm of the aristocracy matched, even surpassed, that of the general public. Law was acclaimed as a genius and a blessing to France.

The company was called the Mississippi Company. Crozat's charter to operate in Louisiana was revoked and given to Law. The Scotchman's interest in the Mississippi country was very real. He personally set in motion all the initial plans, and selected Bienville for his governor.

Like all promoters he refused to believe anything evil about the dreams he dreamed. It must be recognized that at this time the example of another nation which had grown fabulously wealthy by speculating in American trade was still a fresh memory. Spain was on the decline in 1716, but her exploits of the two previous centuries had been prodigious. Had Law's company speculated less, and concerned itself more with the business of bringing the produce of the New World to European markets, it could have known success.

"You will not succeed in Louisiana," declared Crozat, fresh from his own failure. Pointing to the squabbling of his administrators, the obstinacy of Bienville (who believed he should be governor), and the lying reports which the priest Hennepin and the carpenter Penicaut had published, he declared the Louisiana country to be a desolate land, without riches or reward for its exploiter.

But Law reasoned that Crozat's failure was due to picking fools for administrators, and he chose to believe the reports of Penicaut. Furiously, he dismissed the returned governor, l'Epinay, who cursed the new land in response to Law's eager questions.

He engaged recruiters to get immigrants. Contraband salt dealers were the first to be sent out. His first convoys also included an engineer named de la Tour, who would be chief. A second engineer he detained to instruct fully in the kind of colonial city he wanted built. A city that would be consistent with his propaganda, and over-all promotion. The site he left to Bienville, whom he trusted implicitly. Specifically he ordered a church, a building for administration, a governor's mansion, two barracks, a prison, and a general shop.

". . . and call it New Orleans," he instructed the engineer, Adrian de Pauger.

Call it New Orleans because it must be established in the

minds of everybody that this was a crown colony; coupling the colonial capital with the Regent's name was the proper association. No Indian names such as given Biloxi, Mobile, and Natchitoches already established, which would not sell a share of stock to Parisians.

Consistent with this policy of associating the city with the Crown in every conceivable way, Law also ordered the names for the first streets. A wide, important one would also be called for the Regent—Orleans street. There would also be a Chartres, for now the Regent had a son who bore that title. (Law also knew upon which side his bread was buttered.)

A Bourbon street too—the Duke of Bourbon was one of the Bank's best customers, and one of its finest examples of success. Bourbon made enough out of Law's enterprises to rebuild a chateau at Chantilly, complete with a zoo and a race track. He imported 150 horses from England, and gave a party for the Regent's daughter there which lasted five days. A Bourbon street to be sure!

Burgundy street too—the little king's father was the Duke of Burgundy. Get the king's name in too—better make it Saint Louis; it'll sound better, and it'll please the clergy too. We want a favorable reaction from every quarter. Might as well have a Saint Ann street too. It's a popular aristocratic name—besides the women of the court are coming to the Bank more and more. They are coming to Law's home in the Place Vendome, too. Get a Vendome street in also, Pauger is told. The disgusting old General Vendome has been dead since 1712—but it's a good name, and Law's address too. It's more subtle than using his name. He has to stay in the background, but he ought to be unmistakably identified with the project. The people are hailing him as a blessing; the street address will suffice.

Conti street is to be included, and a Condé also. Always remember it is a royal colony; everything we are doing is in the king's name. The Royal Bourbons—work that name in conspicuously. Let's see, who was the first Bourbon? The Count of Clermont. Well, stick him in somewhere.

And the royal bastards—hum-m, they're still influential. To be sure the Regent hates du Maine, but it will be explained to him that personalities cannot be allowed to enter a business proposition. That Comte de Toulouse, the other bastard, he is important in the navy. One of the ships at La Rochelle is named for him. There will also be a Toulouse street, Monsieur de Pauger.

Perhaps it was Law, but more probably it was de Pauger

who placed a royal bastard on either side of Orleans. The poor Duke of Orleans was ever combing Louis XIV's bastards out of his hair. Even so, the manner of associating Toulouse, Orleans, and Dumaine streets in the city plan is a remarkably accurate rendition of the set-up at court. And separating Dumaine and Toulouse from Orleans by a saint street on either side must have been the work of de Pauger—certainly such conservatism is not characteristic of John Law.

De Pauger must have been ordered to draw a proposed map of the city before he ever left, for one was printed in the Paris "Mercure" in 1719—along with beautiful landscapes of Louisiana, views of docile Indian braves kneeling before happy Frenchmen, and dreamy-eyed Indian maidens lounging around. In his promotion, John Law didn't miss a bet. Besides encouraging investors, he had to interest colonists; and he got some good ones, along with his motley band of ex-convicts, beggars, and salt bootleggers.

Adrian de Pauger's earliest map is dated September 1, 1723. This was three years after Law's ruin, but the streets that could not have been named for any other reason than for the advancement of his high pressure promotion remained; and still remain—for the most part—until this day.

One other development of Law's enterprises may have occasioned the name of another Vieux Carré street. His Bank absorbed the so-called Farmers-General of France. These were syndicates who purchased from the crown the privilege of collecting taxes. They reaped their profits from the difference between what they paid for the privilege, and what they could mulct out of the wretched French peasants. That the members of the syndicates almost invariably became enormously wealthy indicates how successful was the harvest of these vultures. Among the most powerful tax farmers at the time of Law were the four Paris brothers, who were natives of the province of Dauphiné. In many ways Law sought to appease these "financiers" after his operations had gobbled up their racket. The eldest of the quartet and their leader, Paris Duvernay, was granted a large concession in the Louisiana country on the Mississippi opposite Manchac. In the end, the Paris brothers were foremost in bringing about the collapse of Law. The Farmers-General system was reinstated.

It is unlikely that Dauphiné street was named for the Dauphin of France. Eight-year-old Louis XV had no dauphin in 1718. Neither was there an heiress, or dauphine. In view of the Paris brothers of Dauphiné, who were active in the Farmers-General after the fall of Law, the evidence that the name originates from them seems most reasonable. Anyway, it first appears on the Brutin map of 1728, spelled Dauphiné.

The Regent was enchanted with the success of Law's system. Because of a slight war with Spain, which the Duke du Maine had precipitated to bring about the downfall of his regency, the Duke of Orleans needed even more money than Law was printing. It seemed to him that credit based on specie could be increased to credit based on all France. Anyway, he ordered more money printed, just as one would order more letterheads. The end was inevitable. Law claimed he was "forced to deviate from true principles." The Duke of Orleans complained to his council that "he (Law) deserved to be hanged." The Duke of Saint Simon, in his Memoirs, expresses an opinion that "Law was not blameless; but Orleans, by forcing him to print so many millions, precipitated him into the abyss."

41

It seems plain, however, that John Law would never have been permitted to operate so novel a system of finance in his time for any other government than that of the Duke of Orleans' regency; and the character of the Regent who permitted its introduction made its ultimate success impossible. It is interesting to this story of New Orleans only in that it gave the city its beginning.

But in the light of what is now known about inflation, it is amusing that this John Law—who is credited with being the inventor of inflation—could never understand it. He became furious with the tradespeople in Paris who raised their prices, as he cheapened the money. He envisioned, for the nation that operated under his system, a land of reduced taxes, no tolls, and every comfort. He ordered barracks built for troops stationed in the provinces. This was new. Always the soldiers were billeted upon the people. (The fact that New Orleans has a Barracks street in its old quarter can be attributed to one dream of Law that materialized.)

One day—during Law's bubble—the young king gave a wad of paper francs to one of his footmen. Historians are still looking for that footman. In 1717 Law obtained a decree ordering servants to get certificates from their masters when leaving their employ, and to find new employment within four days—or else be banished to Louisiana. He secured colonists that way.

Law fled from France in 1720. Instead of wiping out the deficit of Louis XIV, he and the Duke of Orleans doubled it in four years. The reform administration was marching backwards.

The Duke of Orleans—that carousing royal disciple of wine, women and inflation—only lived long enough to turn over a very roughly used France to its young king. Louis XV reached his legal majority of thirteen in 1723. Later that same year the Duke of Orleans died with what has been termed a well-earned stroke of apoplexy. He breathed his last in the arms of one of his mistresses. It would have been unusual had he died anywhere else.

Six years later John Law died in Vienna, as impoverished as the nation he had seduced. Catherine Knollys, Madame Law, remained in Paris when her husband fled. Among other things, she wanted to settle a 10,000-franc butcher bill. She never saw Law again, and neither did the butcher. And—who knows—did Bienville, to whom Law was a friend in need no matter whatever else he was, name Lake St. Catherine for the lady love of his greatest benefactor? (Lake St. Catherine touches the land area of modern New Orleans on its northeast.)

So ended the man for whom the city of New Orleans was named, and the man who fastened that name—and its first street names—upon it. So, too, was hurried along the end of the French monarchy, by whose royal decree it all came to pass.

Tchoupitoulas –
More Than a Street

TCHOUPITOULAS —

MORE THAN A STREET

> *One morning a policeman found a dead*
> *horse lying in the street at the corner of*
> *Common and Tchoupitoulas streets.*
> *He took out his notebook to record the in-*
> *cident. After several futile efforts to spell*
> *Tchoupitoulas he grabbed the horse by the*
> *tail and pulled it a block down the street.*
> *"Dead horse in the street at the corner of*
> *Common and Magazine," he wrote.*
> —Old New Orleans Anecdote

*T*HE word Tchoupitoulas has been as much of a problem
to historians and etymologists. For them no simple solu-
tion, such as the policeman's, is available. Tchoupitoulas
cannot be sidetracked in discussing any phase of New Orleans history, because no name takes in more of the territory which is the present city; no native word appears more
ancient.

And Tchoupitoulas is one of the longest streets in the
city of today.

47

But that policeman needn't have been so concerned over the spelling of the word. Few early historians, map-makers, and recorders of the minutes of the Illustrious Cabildo ever bothered very much. Tchoupitoulas has been found spelled a score of different ways.

Numerous, too, have been explanations of its origin. "It was the name of a tribe of Indians . . . it means fish-hole-road . . . it means mudfish people . . . that a Frenchman came upon an Indian fishing, and when he inquired of his luck, the Indian replied in French, 'Choupic ques tous la.'—meaning that the choupics (mudfish) were all there. Whereupon the French gave the name of Tchoupitoulas to the bayou and the Indians living nearby."

The word first appears as the name of the settlement or plantation of the Chauvin brothers on the east bank of the Mississippi, across from Nine Mile Point. That means the Tchoupitoulas Settlement was nine miles above the St. Louis Cathedral. Application for this concession of land was filed by Joseph Chauvin de Lery in March 1719, just one year after the establishment of New Orleans.

A more primitive form of Tchoupitoulas is Chapitoulas. And its origin? That is as obscure as the wintry mists which so often cloaked that tiny settlement which had been given it for a name. Nobody knows to what Indian dialect Chapitoulas belongs.

In a scholarly analysis, Dr. William A. Reed reasons that if the word is Choctaw it might perhaps be a compound of "hatcha" (river), "pit" (at), and "itoula" (reside);—or literally, "Those Who Reside At The River."

This is a sound analogy, and it is the nearest approximation of the origin of Chapitoulas that may ever be known.

The Chauvin's Chapitoulas Settlement on the Mississippi extended back and included the headwaters of a stream. Geologists surmise that, at one time, this stream joined the river, and was—in effect—another mouth of the Mississippi. Its course is traced along the ridges of Metairie and Gentilly to the neighborhood of the Chef Menteur. Ridges are tell-tale evidence of a flowing stream through an alluvial terrain.

Another crumb of evidence in support of this geological supposition is the earliest mention of Bayou St. John. In 1699 Penicaut states that the Indian name for the bayou was Choupicatcha. In Choctaw this word means Mudfish River. Penicaut gives the fore part, "Choupique" in French; leaving the rest, "atcha," dangling in the native tongue. A better rendition of the word would have been Shupic Hatcha. The Choctaw name for minor streams was bayuk (bayou), but this one they called a river!

Bayou St. John, incidentally, was an insignificant interloper in the waterway system of which Bayous Metairie and Sauvage were the important members. Bayou St. John has no banks, and is believed to be the result of a fault in the earth's surface at one time. Similar bankless streams in the neighborhood are Bayou Bienvenu and the Chef Menteur.

It is conceivable that the fault, when it occurred, may also have shut off the Choupicatcha from the Mississippi. Certainly the stream could not reasonably have received its soubriquet of Mudfish River until after it had been diverted from the main river, became sluggish and otherwise inviting to the fish for whom the Indians called it. Sluggish streams are favored habitats of the choupiques.

In southern Louisiana this curious fish is still called by

its Choctaw-French name of choupique. Elsewhere it is known as the bowfin and grindle. The Louisiana Department of Conservation has this to say about the choupique:

> *"This ancient and remarkable fish dates back in its family history to the time of the Dinosaurs, and is today the single living member of an entire order of fish. . . . "The choupique is a nest builder, the male constructing a home and caring for the eggs and young. This specie, because of the peculiar structure of its swim bladder is able to breathe air in the same manner as does the gar. Choupiques are astonishingly tough . . . not only will they continue to live in what is practically liquid mud, but they have actually been plowed up in the lowland fields of Louisiana, weeks after the flood waters have fallen and when the land has become dry enough for cultivation to begin."*

Like the gar fish, the choupiques prey on other fish and have been known to cut a two-pound trout in half with a single snap of powerful jaws. They grow two feet in length, and without doubt are the only fish in the world that can be fished for with a pick and shovel; and they actually have been in Louisiana. Choupiques are edible but it is necessary to be extraordinarily hungry.

There is no relationship between the name Chapitoulas and the name Choupicatcha other than close proximity; the headwaters of the stream was on the Chapitoulas concession.

But to Dr. Reed it becomes clear that a blending of these two place names has resulted in the word Tchoupitoulas! In 1723, four years after Penicaut distinguishes a Choupicatcha, mention is made of a Bayou Chapitoulas. Another Frenchman writes of a Bayou Tchoupic, identifying it as a branch of Bayou St. John. Then, twenty years after he had recorded the stream as Choupicatcha, Penicaut calls it Bayou Chupic.

Here were certainly ingredients for a blending, and on Carlos Trudeau's Spanish map of 1798 the Shupic Hatcha of the Choctaws is plainly named Tchoupitoulas Bayou. There was the name perpetuated!

Now consider what this French juggling and Spanish interpretation have done to the noble Indians, who if they were Choctaws were the Chapitoulas—or Those Who Reside At The River. Fastening upon them the name of Tchoupitoulas gives to these poor redskins the bewildering literal definition of Mudfish Who Reside!

Nowhere does history mention these Indians as still existing in the neighborhood when the French came. Perhaps, as a tribe, they were already extinct before the arrival of LaSalle and Iberville and Bienville. But any possible stragglers who remained to learn what these early French historians and Spanish mapmakers came to call them must have hastened off into extinction on the double quick. Mudfish Who Reside! Ugh!!

Another recent writer prints a theory that the stream which Penicaut names the Choupicatcha and Bayou Chupic was the Indians' Shupic Hatcha, or Mudfish River. But he makes no connection with Shupic Atcha and Chapitoulas, stating only that the Chapitoulas Indians lived at the one-time junction of the stream at the Mississippi.

He further states that the Chapitoulas were the Mudfish People. But in Choctaw the word for people is goula, or ougoula. Hence the Bayougoulas were the Bayou People; the Pascagoulas, the Bread People; and so on. Mudfish

People would be Shupicgoula. This theory becomes untenable.

Perhaps the four Chauvin brothers who established themselves at the Chapitoulas could have thrown more light upon this word than is now known. But the Chauvins were illiterate. It is said that Nicholas Chauvin de Lafrenniere learned to read and write four months after arriving in Louisiana. But such an education would scarcely have included the ability to translate the curious name of his residence from its obscure, unknown native tongue into his so newly acquired knowledge of written French.

The word was probably learned from the Indians, pronounced in either Choctaw or Mobilian (the jargon used for general communication between the French and all the tribes), then repeated with a French accent to a Spaniard whose knowledge of French was shaky. The earliest known spellings of the plantation are: Choupitoulas, Tchoupitoulas, Chapitoulas, Chapitoula, Le Village des Chapitoulas, Chapitoulas . . . The recurrent persistence of the form, Chapitoulas, indicates it to be the way the word was spoken.

The Chauvin plantation was directly beyond the huge grant of Bienville's, which extended along the river from the present line of Common street to Monticello street in Carrollton. This whole area was called The Chapitoulas. The Chauvins' settlement was known as l'Habitation Chapitoulas. The probability is that all of the area which is now New Orleans was the domain, or hunting ground, of the Chapitoulas Indians—Those Who Reside At The River.

The riverfront of Bienville's concession was known in colonial time as the Chapitoulas (or Tchoupitoulas) Coast.

The road which ran parallel with the river was the Tchou-pitoulas Road. This is Tchoupitoulas street in New Orleans today, five and a half miles in length.

The Chauvins' was a sizable settlement. In 1726 its population included forty-five whites, three hundred and sixty-five Negro slaves, and eleven Indian slaves. There were forty-five horses, and eight hundred parcels of land were under cultivation. In 1726 a census of New Orleans revealed eight hundred and eighty settlers and only ten horses.

Of the four Chauvins, three remained and figured prominently in New Orleans history. Like the LeMoynes, Iberville and Bienville, they attached titular designations to their names. By these they are best known. The first to arrive was Joseph Chauvin, who called himself De Lery. There is a Delery street in New Orleans today. There is also a Lafrenniere street for Nicholas Chauvin de Lafrenniere, but none for Louis Chauvin, called de Beaulieu.

There were two ways for the farmers of the Tchoupitoulas Plantation to get their produce to the people in New Orleans,—by way of the Tchoupitoulas Road, or via Bayou Choupic and the ridge road which was its bank.

The latter was shorter. It became the way to and from the Farm of the Chauvins, and both the bayou and the road came to be called Metairie Bayou and Metairie Road—the bayou and road which lead to the farm, or *métairie,* of the Chauvins. Trudeau's map of 1798 which named a Bayou Tchoupitoulas, also listed a Metairie Road. Upon subsequent maps, the ancient Shupic Hatcha of the Indians was named Bayou Metairie, after the colonial road built on its bank.

Traces of Bayou Metairie still exist in New Orleans as

the lagoon aside Metairie Cemetery and the lagoon along City Park Avenue near Bayou St. John. City Park Avenue was formerly part of Metairie Road and was so called until Civil War time. Here was where the Metairie Road joined the Bayou Road, which led into the city; and here is where the Metairie Bayou joined Bayou St. John. The roads still join but the bayous do not.

Here, also, Bayou Metairie, or the Shupic Hatcha, continued eastward to the gulf. Its continuation was named Bayou Sauvage. Earliest colonial maps show them joined. Roughly, this connection parallels Grand Route St. John— a street which continued Bayou Road to Bayou St. John. Originally, these two streets were one and the same; and today, as separate thoroughfares, each shares part of the name of the one-time single street:—The Grand Route To Bayou St. John.

Just as Metairie Road conferred its name on its bayou, so was Bayou Sauvage also called Bayou Gentilly, for the road on its bank.

There is absolutely no mystery about the origin of Gentilly. Mathurin and Pierre Dreux were attracted to Louisiana by John Law's propaganda. Mathurin, it is said, helped lay out New Orleans. Given a choice of concessions, he selected the high ground along Bayou Sauvage where he was joined by his brother. Like the Chauvins at Tchoupitoulas, the Dreux' prospered. They named their plantation Gentilly, because they had come from the commune in the department of the Seine of that name. In colonial New Orleans these two were known as the Sieurs of Gentilly. Their vast tract was later divided among children, and then grandchildren; but the name which they gave it is still retained by the suburban neighborhood, which once were the acres of the Sieurs of Gentilly. U. S. Highway 90 is still Gentilly Road, and in the Gentilly Terrace neighborhood is also Dreux Avenue.

But as for Tchoupitoulas, it is astonishing that the word has retained this spelling of 1798. The rough treatment it received from the French was matched by the Spaniards, as the minutes of the Illustrious Cabildo will testify.

On one day, October 30, 1789, it is spelled Choupitoula and Choucpictoula—both in the same handwriting. This proves nothing except that Spaniards could not be trusted to spell the word the same in the afternoon as they did in the morning. Furthermore, it does not appear that this particular scribe was at all influenced by precedent, even Spanish precedent. For nine years prior to this, on January 3, in the minutes of the Cabildo, Tchoupitoulas is preserved for posterity spelled Chapitular. This may have been a winter spelling of the word.

But how Tchoupitoulas is spelled, and where it originates are not the first problem for the visitor to New Orleans when first confronted with this string of thirteen vowels and consonants. How do you pronounce it?

Here also there are several versions. Mostly, it depends upon what section of the five and a half miles of Tchoupitoulas street one is standing when he wants to say it. The street runs through Negro neighborhoods and it runs through the Irish Channel; it also runs along the riverfront, haunt of sea-faring men from all nations.

It can be pronounced: CHOP-it-TOO-lus.

It is also heard: CHA-A-AP-a-TO-loose.

It is even rendered: choppie-TOla.

Growing Pains

GROWING PAINS

*O*NCE the settlement they called New Orleans was planted in the Louisiana wilderness, it clung tenaciously to life. And it survived.

But survival wasn't easy. Just a year after its beginning hurricane winds and flooding brown waters of the Mississippi, each in turn, sought to blow it away and wash it away. Yet, withstanding these furies, it stayed put. Thus, this city they called New Orleans achieved the distinction of being the first important place of human habitation in the valley of the Mississippi. There on the river end of the ancient portage it stood, in a swampy low region where—and it is a matter of historical record—even the Indians wouldn't live.

Bienville's problems on the receiving end of John Law's operations were multiple. Shiploads multiplied by shiploads of settlers were dumped upon him. Dauphin Island, disembarkation port for the convoys from LaRochelle, all but sank into Mobile Bay under the weight of convicts, beggars, and unfortunate victims of a despotic regime in France. These formed the bulk of the colonists sent to populate Louisiana.

Some were consigned. Law's own huge four-square-league concession in the Arkansas country was provided with two hundred Germans. Sixty settlers arrived for Paris Duvernay's grant opposite Manchac on the river. Seventy for De La Houssie—his concession was in the ancient country of the Houmas Indians, near the Red River junction; and sixty more for De La Harpe, whose land was at Natchitoches. At Natchez was St. Reneyes representing a group of St. Malo investors—there were settlers for him and for others too. And one of the convoys specifically indicated sixty-eight for "the new town of New Orleans."

In 1722 New Orleans took the failure of Law in its infant, but none the less lusty, stride. It is noteworthy at this time, that among the commissioners sent to inventory the colony was one Jacques De La Chaise. A street would be named for his grandson one day. These commissioners ordered the seat of government moved to New Orleans. Biloxi had been burned down by that sergeant's pipe, anyway. Remember?

Reports of these "efficiency experts" are judged to have resulted in the ill-advised recall of Bienville. Perrier replaced him. There is a Perrier street in New Orleans, but in the time of Governor Perrier all there seemed to be was Indian trouble. This was the time of the Natchez Massacre. Fort Rosalie—named for the wife of Pontchartrain—was destroyed. For mutual protection the scattered settlers drew closer to New Orleans, among whom were the Germans on Law's Arkansas concession. They reestablished at a point upriver from the settlement; and the region came to be called the German Coast—or Côte des Allemands. The present village of Des Allemands remains a permanent marker for this pioneer development.

Meanwhile, in New Orleans, certain other streets had acquired names because of their locations and associations in the community. Such was Rue de la Quai; or Levee street, as it was called until 1870, when its name became Decatur. Due to the action of the river in altering its course, it was no longer on the levee.

A street upon which the Ursuline nuns built their first convent had been called, prior to this construction, St. Adrian street. Adrian de Pauger named it for himself and his patron saint. So far as is known, this is all that Pauger ever received for his labors in behalf of New Orleans, this brief distinction of having a St. Adrian street in the street nomenclature. Incidentally, Pauger soon afterwards was able to qualify for sainthood—in one essential, anyway— when he died in 1726. The first geographer of New Orleans is buried in the city he planned, and more recently his name has been reinstated in the nomenclature. There is a Pauger street in New Orleans now.

St. Adrian was changed, first to St. Ursula, and then again to the name it now bears, Ursulines. Another street was first called Arsenal because the arsenal was there; then Hospital, for similar reason. It was Hospital for one hundred and eighty years, until rechristened Governor Nicholls street. Civil War Hero Francis Tillou Nicholls has a lonely fate among Vieux Carré streets, in eternal association with Dumaine, Toulouse, the Duke of Orleans, et al. Placing this patriotic Irish-American in this stuffy Bourbon company—even in name only—is a dubious honor.

Bienville was hustled back to replace Perrier and stop the Indian fighting, an assignment which he accomplished with his usual efficiency. Ironically, Bienville's last notable service to Louisiana was of exactly the same nature as was his very first—settling the trouble with the Indians. Soon after peace was established, this extraordinary man left Louisiana—never to return—in May of 1743. His was a fifty-four-year struggle to build for France an empire in the Mississippi valley. He founded an empire, but it was not to be for France.

The Marquis de Vaudreuil replaced Bienville. A Marquis for governor! Louisiana was looking up. There used to be a Vaudreuil street in New Orleans, but it fell into the discard during one of the street name shuffles, of which the city has had several. The Marquis, himself, very soon after his arrival, shuffled off to Canada to administer affairs of that colony. Kerlerec, a naval officer who happened to be stranded ashore, became governor. His was a brief, peaceless, and inconsequential administration.

It is therefore paradoxical that two streets in modern New Orleans, which Bernard Marigny originally named Peace and History, have been changed to Kerlerec—Kerlerec, who knew no peace and made little history. Even the Indians called this blundering, unskilled administrator Chef Menteur, meaning, as does the waterway east of New Orleans, Chief Liar.

This waterway, which, together with the Rigolets, empties Lake Pontchartrain into the gulf, was termed Chief Liar among streams because its current deceptively flows either way with the tide. In the inadequate language of the Indians, Chef Menteur means, "big liar," "one who deceives," or "untrustworthy one." And that was the Indians' opinion of the governor.

In justice to Kerlerec, his bad reputation was not entirely of his own making. He had enemies who helped. M.

Rochemore, the civil administrator, from the day of his arrival until his recall, spent his every waking hour scheming to discredit the governor. In this his wife was a great help; and one of the things which bothered Kerlerec most of all were the risqué songs attacking him which Madame Rochemore was continually writing and circulating. The Rochemores kept poor Kerlerec continually up in the air; consequently it is singularly appropriate that Kerlerec street in New Orleans today also goes up in the air in three places! There are that many gaps in the street's course, over which it must hurdle, to complete its assigned length from Chartres street to North Dorgenois.

Even when he was relieved of his Louisiana job, Kerlerec's troubles did not cease. Back in France he was thrown in the Bastille. There were some vague charges about being responsible for losing the French and Indian war, which had been going on during his administration.

Director General D'Abadie performed the governing chores after the departure of Kerlerec. There was little general directing to be done in Louisiana following the war which had lost for France all of her North American possessions east of the Mississippi River, except the Island of Orleans. M. Kerlerec in the Bastille notwithstanding, Louis XV lost this war through uninterested neglect. Neglect which Mr. William Pitt, the English Prime Minister did not share. (Louis XV was more interested in Madame Pompadour. There is a Pitt street in uptown New Orleans today, but no where in town is there a Louis XV street—nor a Madame Pompadour street.

D'Abadie died in 1766, and a man named Aubry became the administer of what affairs there were. Aubry was a political zombie. Zombies are said to be characters who should be dead, but walk around anyway. They shouldn't do anything, considering their condition; however, they will do anything at all that anybody at all directs them to do. This was Aubry's record.

He was appointed to rule a French colony which had been transferred to Spain. As French administrator he didn't do anything; and whatever the first two Spanish administrators told him to do, he did. There is an Aubry street in New Orleans, also a D'Abadie street, but tucked in carefully where they do not show.

The record of France in Louisiana is characterized by a persistent effort upon the part of that nation to give the country away to anybody—except back to the Indians. It was given to Antoine Crozat in 1712, and to John Law in 1716. In 1763 it was given to Spain; and finally, after Napoleon had taken it back again, it was "given" to the United States for 4¢ an acre.

The French city of New Orleans was shocked when it learned it had been given to Spain. However, in the thirty-seven years of Spanish domination in Louisiana, that nation's costs are roughly equivalent to what the United States paid to buy the country outright. All Spain ever received in return for her expenditures was a buffer state between her rich Mexico and the restless Anglo-Saxons on the Atlantic seaboard. Spain should have been shocked when Louisiana was given to her!

The French Orleanians had recovered from their shock when Don Antonio de Ulloa arrived. They didn't like this Spanish governor. Also, they didn't like his wife. Furthermore, they didn't like a lot of Catalonian wine which had also arrived in place of their beloved Bordeaux. About 600 citizens assembled and ran Ulloa out. Historians do not explain what happened to the Catalonian wine. This resistance in New Orleans in 1768 marks the first revolutionary movement of Americans against a European power. Don Antonio never returned. However, in the 1850's, when streets were laid out in back-of-town New Orleans, his name popped up as the label of one of those streets!

Leader of this revolution of 1768 was Nicholas Chauvin de Lafrenniere, attorney general of the colony and son of the first Lafrenniere who had come with Bienville, and who settled with his brothers at Chapitoulas. Others whose names deserve a place in the cast of this drama were: Faucault, John and Joseph Milhet, Petit, Noylan, Mazan, Boisblanc, and Villere. All were either banished or executed for their leadership in the rebellion; yet few of their names are street names today. On the other hand, the name of the leader of the avenging army which Spain sent to New Orleans is—there is an O'Reilly street!

To crush the revolt, to punish the upstart city, to erase the insult to his Catholic Majesty, Carlos of Spain, Don Alexander O'Reilly arrived with a force which—man to man—outnumbered the male population of New Orleans. The rebels gulped, and were willing to let bygones be bygones. Not so O'Reilly. Historians have been trying to understand and explain the harsh cruelty of "Bloody O'Reilly" ever since the firing squad's volley rang out over the broad Esplanade, reechoed across the river, and was swallowed into the October silence. Leaders of the Revolution of 1768 slumped to the earth.

The Spanish officer in charge of the musketeers—legend says he was Captain Jacinto Panis—advanced toward the still forms. All dead. The sentence had been carried out.

No historian—or anybody else—has ever thought to report whether Captain Panis particularly noticed Joseph Milhet lying there with Lafrenniere and the other partisans; or what the good captain thought about when eight years later he married his widow!

Margarethe Wiltz—the legend insists—never knew that her Jacinto had officiated at her Joe's shooting. She named a street after this second husband; Jackson avenue was first called Grand Route Panis. But the only thing that ever had poor Joe's name on it was that Spanish bullet.

It remained for Bernard Marigny, thirty-six years later, to immortalize all these heroic Frenchmen with a street name. Marigny's land adjoined the Esplanade, and that section of this drill ground and promenade where Lafrenniere and his lieutenants were placed for execution is today the beginning of Frenchmen street. The street of the Frenchmen, Marigny called it; and regardless of how much their dislike for Ulloa precipitated their action; regardless, too, of how much their distaste for Catalonian wine; it was for rebelling against Spain that they died, and France refused to intercede in their behalf. It was for Freedom that their lives were forfeited.

Today, mostly Italians and Irishmen live on Frenchmen street.

So Spanish rule began, and began also a procession of Spanish governors: Onzaga, Galvez, Miro, Carondelet, Gayoso, Salcedo, and Casa Calvo. A New Orleans street is named for every one—and for Galvez, for whom the Texas city of Galveston is also named, there is even a telephone exchange in New Orleans!

The Spaniards themselves named few streets, but they had a lot of trouble with those they sought to label. The city had grown on both sides. A new street on its lower extremity was first called Customhouse—or Duana—street. The customhouse was there. But the soldiers were quartered there also, so it was decided that, maybe, the street should be called Street of the Quarters—*Quartel* (in Spanish) and *Quartier* (in French). Soldiers were evidently more important than customs then; anyway, somebody built a new customhouse on the opposite side of town. So quickly that street was named New Customhouse street. Later, people began calling the street where the soldiers were Garrison street, then finally, Barracks which it has remained.

Much later, in 1897, New Customhouse street ran into a little trouble for five of the fifty-three blocks of its length. Those were the blocks which ran through the notorious red light district! In 1911, the street's name for its whole length was piously altered to Iberville, its present name.

Another great problem of the Spaniards was to keep from getting lost in the back-of-town sections. It was swampy there. The present Marais street was so called because this street, only ten blocks back from the river, *was* the marais—or swamp. Upon the portage—Bayou Road was no exception in rainy, river flood time—the Spaniards, first fastened the sobriquet, "Portage of the Lost"—or "Perdido," in Spanish the past participle of the verb, "lose." The neighborhood of North Galvez from Bayou Road to the Carondelet Canal shows a Perdido Road on some maps. Perdido became a popular name for streets which were apt to get lost under water and in New Orleans' early days every street which ran back a dozen blocks was a possible Perdido street. One such street has formally acquired the name of Perdido, and is still so called.

Fires were another problem to the Spaniards. The French were always having unfortunate relations with fire, ever since they burned the old Biloxi Indian to a crisp as a friendly gesture. The Spaniards acquired this misfortune when they acquired Louisiana. Don José Vincente Nunez, paymaster of the army, seems to have acquired more than his share. On March 21, 1788, he got a fire started in his home on Chartres and Toulouse streets that was so big nobody had to go to it. It came to almost everybody; four-fifths of the town went up in smoke.

Six years later the French rallied to regain their championship. In a house on Royal street, a small blaze, tended by Frenchmen, got out of hand and burned down 212 buildings.

Today many Orleanians term the old city "French Quarter." The sight-seeing hawkers never call it anything else. But as a matter of fact, due to this fiery double-header, plus the normal ravages of time, most of the notable buildings in the Vieux Carré are either the construction of the Spaniards—or the WPA. The French Market, for instance, was wholly rebuilt in 1936.

Ville Gravier, across the commons, rose from the ashes of these fires. And across the Atlantic Ocean, some other French fireworks caused the establishment of forts and ramparts around the city. Both of these incidents provided New Orleans with additional street names.

Francisco Luis Hector, Baron de Carondelet, was Spanish governor in Louisiana during the time of the French Revolution. He strengthened Forts St. Louis, St. John and Burgundy; and built Fort St. Charles and Fort St. Ferdinand—and he added a rampart at the back of town. As military installations these fortifications were ludicrous.

They were intended to impress the Frenchmen and keep them in, rather than repel any trouble from an outside source; every one of the forts has provided the city of today with a street name—and the Rampart too!

Carondelet built other things besides puny fortresses. He dug a canal which extended Bayou St. John to the very back door of the city. The council—the Very Illustrious Cabildo—considered this such an achievement that it passed a resolution naming it the Canal of Carondelet. He dug another ditch from Fort St. Louis, at the Tchoupitoulas Gate, through the city commons back into the swamp. The Very Illustrious Cabildo took notice of this, and did nothing at all about naming it. It is a street now, and called Canal street, although its name does not come from this ditch.

Directly beyond the commons lay the huge Jesuits' plantation, with its eighty-four arpent frontage on the river. An arpent is an old French measure of land which varied in value with the locality. In Louisiana and French Canada (the only regions in North America where the measure was used) an arpent was 180 French feet. And just as a French heel is more than an ordinary heel, so is a French foot more than the ordinary foot; 100 French feet are equivalent to 106¼ feet. All concessions in Louisiana were in arpents, and all old titles in New Orleans were in French feet. In the closing years of the French domination, the Jesuits plantation reverted to the Crown when that order was suppressed.

Banishing the Jesuits from Louisiana and confiscating their property are among the things that D'Abadie and Aubry did wrong. Not only did they lead New Orleans into jumping the gun by ten years when they expelled the order from the colony in 1763, but the action was illegal because it was taken after Louisiana had been secretly transferred to Spain. In later years the fathers of the Society of Jesus returned to Louisiana; and today, on Loyola street—named for the founder of the Jesuit order—one may ride across the land which was once their colonial plantation, and across town, to the campus of the impressive Jesuit institution of Loyola University.

At the public sale of the Jesuit plantation, which followed its confiscation, six purchasers bought. In 1900, James S. Zacharie reported to the Louisiana Historical Society that the price paid by them amounted to $180,000. Today few corner lots in this area, which comprises the commercial district of New Orleans, would come under this figure. The six purchasers were: Pradel, Larivée, Grenier, Bonrepos, Soulet, and Livaudais.

Captain John Pradel got the best slice. His seven arpent frontage measured from the commons (Common street) to a line directly through the center of Lafayette Square of today. It was adjacent to the city, separated only by the commons. Captain Pradel's wife was Alexandrina de la Chaise, daughter of the French commissioner. When Pradel died, Alexandrina sold the tract to André Renard, who died and left it to his wife, Marie Josepha Deslonde. Bertrand Gravier fell madly in love with Marie and her arpents. They married; then she died and left her seven arpents to Bertrand. On the last day she made the will, historians slyly point out! Bertrand died before he ever got a chance to make a will. The thirteen acres of arpents were inventoried, and Bertrand's brother John bought them for $2,400. This is about the annual rent of an orange juice stand in the neighborhood today.

Incidentally, John Gravier died a bum.

But it was before his wife died, in 1788 after the first fire, that Bertrand laid off four rows of lots along Tchoupitoulas street—the Royal Road. After the second fire he added more lots. Due to the fires, Bertrand and Marie had a very hot real estate boom. First called Ville Gravier, Bertrand renamed it Faubourg Ste. Marie when his wife died. By this name it continued to be known until long after American domination.

With one exception, the first streets in the Graviers' subdivision were named for landmarks associated with them. One block back from Tchoupitoulas was Magazine, named for the *magazin* or *almazon* (in English we call it warehouse) where Kentucky tobacco and other goods were stored awaiting export. This street was just across the commons from the *magazin,* and its location was identified with it.

The Graviers lived in a square that faced Magazine. It was flanked by the commons (now Common street) and another street named Gravier; and similarly, the name of the street behind their square was called Camp for the huts or encampment of their slaves on that street.

Julian Poydras, writing in defense of the city's claim to the batture twenty-five years after Gravier opened his subdivision, gives himself full credit for the creation of Ville Gravier. After the fire of 1788, Poydras claims he suggested to Bertrand Gravier that he subdivide his estate into a suburb. It took considerable persuasion, Poydras emphasized in his public letter, and he had to promise to buy the first lot. He did, paying $1,000 for his corner site on Tchoupitoulas and the street named for him. Other lots were sold for $400, Poydras added sadly. He hauled bricks from his Pointe Coupee plantation, and declared his to have been the first house raised in the new suburb. In this pamphlet, Poydras further supplied all readers with the information that Bertrand Gravier was a fugitive from his native Bordeaux, where he had been a bankrupt.

Nicholas Girod was another who invested in Gravier's real estate, and the street named Girod marks the location of his holdings.

A legend persists that Julia street is named for a Negro slave. Julia was Poydras' cook, and so good a cook that he gave her her freedom. An odd man, that Poydras, who is said to have presided over the first bank in the Mississippi valley and had the first poem published in the Mississippi valley. Neither has survived.

The only documentary proof that Julia street is actually called for the legendary Julia is the listing in the city directory of a Julia Mathew, a free woman of color. But this Julia lived at 28 Levee (Decatur) street. And in contradiction of the legend is the fact that Julie was the *petit nom* or nick-name, of Julian Poydras. And on early maps Julia street is written Julie.

The single exception to the practice of identifying streets with landmarks was St. Charles. It couldn't have been associated with Fort St. Charles which was on Esplanade and the river, the other side of town. Like the fort, it was named for the King of Spain. And Carondelet was named for the king's governor.

The Baron Carondelet is said to have maintained a hunting lodge on Duck Lake, a mudhole in the vicinity of Carondelet and Poydras streets. His wife, the Baronne, is also reported to have planted a rose garden in Ville Gravier; but, so far as is known, the only thing that took root is her name to the street one block from Carondelet. The street called University Place was named Philippa, in honor of the daughter of the Carondelets. But so far back in the woods at the time of Carondelet's administration, it probably never existed as Philippa, except on the surveyor's maps. As University Place, it gets its name from the Louisiana University, forerunner of Tulane, which was located there.

The indications are that the Graviers acquired the adjoining property of Larivée and a portion of Grenier's. Early maps of Ville Gravier show the upper line of the subdivision at a point just above St. Joseph street. And St. Joseph is named for Bertrand's wife, Marie Josepha Deslonde—the good woman whose first husband thoughtfully acquired the property which the Graviers inherited.

All other streets in the Ville Gravier, or Faubourg Ste. Marie, came later, and must be credited to the American developers on the section.

Creole vs. Kaintock –
...Round One

CREOLE vs. KAINTOCK

— ROUND ONE

*C*HARACTERISTICALLY, young Americans have always returned from wars only long enough to marry the girl, and trek off to new and distant surroundings in their huge land. Such periods of unrest are familiar following the world war of the GI's, and the trench-fighting war of their doughboy fathers. To a lesser degree it applied to the immunes and the "roughriders," when those soldiers of '98 were mustered out of their minor league unpleasantness with the Spaniards. The years following the Civil War saw the "winning of the West"; and America's very first postwar years resulted in the settlement of the Mississippi-Ohio valley.

Statistically, soon after the Revolution, the nation's center of population moved a full fifty miles westward from the Atlantic coast. Before the surrender of the British at Yorktown, settlers beyond the Alleghenies numbered between ten and fifteen thousands. The U. S. census of 1800 reported 380,772 in the territories of Ohio, Kentucky, Tennessee and Mississippi. The latter was a very poor fourth; the great majority of the settlers stopped along the upper waters of the Ohio, Tennessee, and Cumberland river systems. Pittsburgh, Louisville, and Cincinnati on the Ohio; Nashville on the Cumberland; and Knoxville high up the Tennessee River became the metropolises of the new country.

So many people cutting virgin timber, trapping furs, growing Indian corn and wheat and tobacco, and no other way to market than by way of the main street of the continent—the Mississippi River! New Orleans, at the end of the street, began to experience the results which Bienville, her founder, had dreamed for his city.

But in the last years of the Spanish regime at New Orleans, the vanguard of this river commerce experienced difficulties. The Spaniards were fussy about their port. They feared this rising tide of American activity up the river. They clamped excessive duties and annoying restrictions on the Americans. Frequently, whole cargoes were confiscated. For a period the port was closed to the Kentucky rivermen entirely.

This vanguard was no trickle. Between 1800 and 1801, 697 flatboats reached New Orleans. The flatboat was the first craft used on the river, and the last one to give up to steam. At New Orleans they were abandoned, or broken up and the wood sold. Many of the houses in Faubourgs Ste. Marie and Marigny were built of flatboat timber; and many a plank sidewalk laid over gumbo mud was formerly the oaken hull of a sturdy river flatboat.

The New Orleans Creoles' introduction to the river boatmen was no Emily Post affair. They saw the rugged, buckskinned Kentuckians at the riverfront and they were witness to the Spanish inhospitality toward these newcomers. And when the boatmen were shut off from the facilities of the port by the Spanish ruling of 1798, Tchoupitoulas street reechoed with loud and violent threats, complete with picturesque details, that the Kentuckians would return and loot this dad-burned, blankety-blank city of New Orleans.

As ambassadors of good will these first Kentucky rivermen—Kaintocks, the Creoles called them—were as diplomatic as the bleachers at a Sunday ball game late in the season. The Creoles ruled them out as the sort of people they would want to spend the rest of their lives with in the same community. But instead of venting their wrath upon New Orleans, it was the American government at Washington that heard from the frontiersmen. Kentucky and Tennessee, newly admitted to statehood in the 1790's, threatened to secede from the union unless something was done about the situation at New Orleans.

President Thomas Jefferson dispatched Monroe and Livingston to bargain with Napoleon for the Island of Orleans. Louisiana was suddenly French again. Napoleon had taken it back. This buying trip of Messrs. Monroe and Livingston was one of the most successful of all time. Instead of only the Island of New Orleans, the tiny section of the Louisiana territory on the river's east bank upon which was the port of New Orleans, the emissaries returned with title to the whole of Louisiana—approximately a million square miles for less than a nickel an acre.

(In New Orleans, today, streets are named for Jefferson, Monroe, Livingston, Louisiana, and Napoleon.)

Immediately after the purchase, goods shipped through the port of New Orleans jumped fifty percent. Besides the flatboats, keelboats were nosing into the batture at Tchoupitoulas street. For the next thirty years, these craft alone would average a thousand a year at the New Orleans riverfront.

The keelboat was a development of the Kentucky boatmen. A huge skiff it was, pointed at both sides. Its keel—an oak four-by-four—permitted some control of the craft, and gave it its name. The keelboat ranged between 40 and 80 feet in length; with a 7 to 10 foot beam. Steering was by a long oar; usually this was the captain's job, from his station atop the cabin amidship. On each side of this cabin were the cleated runways. Here the crewmen poled and bushwacked, for the feature of the keelboat was that it could make the return trip up the river.

Bushwacking was a maneuver wherein the crew grabbed at bushes and trees along the riverbank, literally clawing their way upstream. It was only effective when the river was high, and the bushes and trees protruded from the boatable water.

Poling and towing with a line on shore were other ways of battling the current of Old Man River. Some sections of the river were more difficult than others, and probably no stretch called for more elbow grease than a section of the Tennessee River that came to be called Muscle Shoals, now the site of the huge hydro-electric plants of TVA.

Flatboatmen returned overland, up the riverbank to Natchez, and from there to Nashville via the Natchez Trace. The Trace, a barely discernible track through the wilderness, went from Natchez to Nashville almost as straight as a crow would fly. The returning boatmen travelled together for protection from Indians and road agents. It was a twenty-day walk, every mile of it beset with danger.

Creole vs. Kaintock—Round One

Usually the flatboatmen were farmers and family men with homes and ties in Kentucky and Tennessee and Ohio. For them the trip to New Orleans was an adventurous, hazardous holiday. But the keelboatmen were professionals. The river was their life. The Keelboat Age was a forty-five-year period in American history, the last decade of which was spent in the upper river after the invasion of the steamboat.

The river was tough. As traffic grew in size and richness, river pirates added to the natural hardships of the voyages. It was tough, but the keelboatmen were tougher. Of all the hardy, rough-and-tumble ferocious frontiersmen with gun and knife, and tooth and claw who carved an empire from the North American wilderness, the keelboatmen possessed those characteristics in most abundance. And they were the kind of guys, who—if you didn't believe it— would make a bloody-nosed issue of the matter. Historians lose no time in conceding them the championship. Usually they were ex-Indian fighters, and recruits to their ranks maintained if not exceeded the rugged constitutions necessary for that line of work.

Life on the keels consisted of much hard work, and long periods of ease and idleness. On each trip the ease and idleness came first, as the current swept the boat down to the warm ports of Natchez Under-The-Hill, and Journey's End at New Orleans.

There was ample supply of food and music and whiskey and women, and all of it was bad. One keelboat cook boasted that he was a cobbler by trade and a Republican by profession. His cooking proved that this must have been so; and he was a typical keelboat cook. Each keelboat had its barrel of Monongahela rye whiskey secured in plain

81

sight amidship. No keelboater would sign on a boat without it, and the privilege of taking a nip with or without a reason.

The music was a type of mountain music that had lost altitude; and the women were the Lorelei who waited in New Orleans to lure them to The Swamp, back-of-town on Girod street.

Perhaps the keelboater's most enjoyable off-duty pastime was fighting. Each boat had its champ, or bully, who wore a red turkey feather as an insignia of his pre-eminence —literally, a chip on his shoulder. The ambition of each boat's bully was to fight another boat's bully. So when several hundred keelboats tied up at Tchoupitoulas street, there were duels of the champs, and then whole crews jumped rival crews. The results were frequently fights with nobody left to watch.

There were two kinds of fights among keelboatmen. The fair fights were limited to simple slugging and kicking. The rough-and-tumble was more spectacular. The wide range of this form of combat can best be gleaned from a law passed in Kentucky in 1811 which limited rough-and-tumble fights to stabbing only.

These bullies and lesser bullies ruined the reputation of keelboatmen for all time among the New Orleans Creoles. In fact they seriously impaired the reputation of all the peoples of the western country, the hated Kaintocks.

Upon occasion the keelboaters delighted in vandalistic attacks upon the Creoles. In the early 1800's a civilized way of life prevailed in New Orleans, and keelboaters appear to have considered civilization sissified. The attack upon Gaetano's circus was notable.

It was a summer night in 1817. Fifty keelboaters, filled

with rye whiskey and indignation toward Creole civilization, descended upon Senor Gaetano's tent show, a block
back from Philippa street in Faubourg Ste. Marie. What
resulted was undoubtedly one of the most spectacular tent
performances in show business. There was audience participation, as Creoles drew cane swords in defense, and
there was keelboatmen participation with clubs and
knives; in fact, there was even wild animal participation,
for the marauders had released the menagerie. The next
morning Senor Gaetano took one look at the mess which
had been his circus, and took the next boat back to his
native Havana. However, the street one block back from
Philippa street (which is now called University Place)
continued to be called Circus street until Civil War time.
It is now South Rampart street.

But such boyish pranks—a la keelboat—did not consti-
tute the boatmen's most enjoyable evenings in town. For
real fun after dark, tired keelboaters repaired to The
Swamp. Ten blocks back from the river on Girod street
were clusters of saloons, dancehalls, gambling dens,
brothels and flop-houses. The boundaries of this oasis of
iniquity began at present-day South Liberty street, and its
six sordid squares of shacks and shanties sprawled further
back into the swamp. That it was called The Swamp is
the solitary honest thing that can be associated with this
lecherous community where the shake-down, the mickey-
finn, and crooked gambling were the rule and not the exception. There everything was cheap, even life.

No city policeman in his right mind ever ventured within extreme shotgun range of this keelboatmen's play-
ground. Here they might booze and gamble and cut up
capers (and also other keelboatmen) to their heart's con-

tent. The red lights of The Swamp continued to beckon with their scarlet glimmers until the steam packets pushed the keelboats back up the river.

Until 1926 there was a Swamp street in New Orleans. But it was the continuation of North White street from Ursulines to Maurepas, with no geographical or moral connection with the keelboaters' snug harbor.

A Creole is a native born Orleanian of French and/or Spanish extraction. The name comes from the Spanish word, *crillo:* meaning, children born in the colonies. In its adjective form, the word qualifies anything and everything owned by or associated with the Creoles. Consequently, there are Creole cooking, Creole horses, Creole music, Creole customs. And there were, of course, Creole slaves.

It is because the slaves owned by the Creoles were so called that the label of Creole has been incorrectly applied to Negroes. The confusion is increased by the slaves of the Creoles themselves, who took great pride in being thus different from the slaves of the Americans. They were different, even in language; and the slaves of the Americans were never permitted at the week-end revelries of the Creole slaves in Congo Square. Congo Square is now Beauregard Square, in front of the Municipal Auditorium.

The animosity toward all Americans that the Kaintock rivermen instilled in the Creoles continued for long years. It tremendously affected the pattern of growth of the city; in ways great and small, serious and amusing. It haunted succeeding generations as the two civilizations teamed to forge a metropolis. Why, in a number of notable instances, Creole streets have never linked up and never shared their names with American streets which continue their length!

As the river traffic boomed, and the wealth of the Mississippi valley poured into New Orleans, Anglo-Saxon investors, capitalists, merchants, and men of commerce were attracted to the city. They found a native population which tolerated them, but plainly disliked them, and whose society snubbed them. The energetic Americans, on the other hand, saw much in the formal, tradition-bound Creoles that they did not like. This, coupled with the coolness of their reception, kept them apart. Thus was begun two factions, two societies, two cities of New Orleans.

During the first decade of the 19th century, the Creole population was augmented by many thousands of refugees from Santo Domingo. The relationship between Americans and Creoles improved only slightly after both fought shoulder to shoulder at the Battle of New Orleans in 1815. The Creoles were the more numerous. In the City Council and in the State Legislature Creole majorities worked against American interests.

Americans were concentrated in the suburb above the old town, the Faubourg Ste. Marie which had been opened after the great fire. American merchants, more speculative and generous with credit, were prospering from the river trade. Although James H. Caldwell had opened his American Theatre on Camp street near Gravier, people had to walk two blocks on rude wooden walks to attend these first presentations of English drama in New Orleans. Not a street above the commons (Canal street) was paved in 1828. Truck gardens surrounded the American Theater which played to standing room only!

It was at about this time that Samuel J. Peters was trying to persuade Bernard Marigny to sell his faubourg below the city to the American syndicate which he headed.

Apparently the Americans reasoned that what they could not do in the Faubourg Ste. Marie, they might accomplish in Faubourg Marigny, which its Creole owner had begun to open for settlement in 1807.

Besides the keelboaters, whom the Creoles hated, there was also the confusion of ownership of the batture in front of the Faubourg Ste. Marie. The batture was several hundred yards of land which the river had deposited between Tchoupitoulas street and itself. When the lawyer, Edward Livingston, arrived in New Orleans in 1803, he saw the activity of the flatboats and the keelboats on the batture, and was surprised to learn that nobody owned it. John Gravier owned the land which fronted on Tchoupitoulas street, and the batture which fronted on the river. Livingston acquired Gravier as a client, and also seems to have acquired the batture as his own property. That is, it was his legal understanding that it was his property, as riparian owner of all river deposits between his client's land and the water line.

When he sought to take possession, there were riots between his workers and the people who used the batture as a public wharf. The court decision of December 18, 1806, gave him title; notwithstanding, the people refused to move away. Governor Claiborne appealed to President Jefferson, who put aside the court decision, termed Livingston a squatter (Violation of Squatters Act of 1807), and ordered U. S. Marshal LeBreton D'Orgenois to remove Livingston.

Livingston got an injunction from the Superior Court of the Territory of Louisiana which declared his removal by U.S. Marshal D'Orgenois to be in contempt of court. He sent his workmen back to work on the batture. Thousands of citizens thereupon went back to rioting, and Livingston's claim simmered down into a long drawn out series of lawsuits and hearings and bitter pamphleteering between himself and now ex-president Thomas Jefferson.

Unquestionably this litigation retarded the development of this section of New Orleans for many years. It certainly influenced Samuel J. Peters, who did everything he could to get Marigny to cooperate in his great plans for developing New Orleans.

Unfortunately for the downtown section of New Orleans, the animosity between Creole and American, and, in this case, additional animosity between a Creole gentleman and his wife, rendered Peters' efforts fruitless. Madame de Marigny was a willful woman but the Creoles won the first round.

Creole vs. Kaintock –
Round Two

CREOLE vs. KAINTOCK

— ROUND TWO

*B*ERNARD XAVIER PHILIPPE DE MARIGNY DE MANDEVLLE is one of the great personalities of New Orleans history. And probably he named more streets than any other man. The story of Bernard Marigny—as he came to be called— is another of those piteous sagas of the rich man's son who was denied nothing. His story ran the usual course; Bernard Marigny ended with nothing.

But life the way Marigny lived it was an enrichment to New Orleans, socially, geographically, and in the flavor of its street nomenclature. Like the buzzing honeybee which hedgehops from flower to flower unknowingly pollinating and directing future growth, so did Marigny's career leave surprising blossoming in its wake. It is not known what fun and pleasure the bee derives from his ordained chores, but Bernard Marigny enjoyed to the fullest every one of the ninety-three years he buzzed around from 1775 to 1868. Even in adversity and penniless poverty he ended his days as he began them—the greatest Creole of them all.

When Bernard was thirteen, his father's house guest was the Duke of Orleans, great-great-grandson of the prince for whom the city had been named. The Duke was in America sitting out the French Revolution, and he was broke. Bernard's father loaned him money with the vague security that the Duke would repay the loan when he became king. It was something of a joke; but Peter Marigny had enough money to joke with.

However, thirty-two years later this Duke of Orleans, Louis Philippe, did become King of France. Then Bernard Marigny was broke, and the matter of the loan was brought up. Thereupon King Louis Philippe repaid Marigny with a complete set of dishes with the King's picture on each and every piece. This was considered a great honor, and also a considerable saving to Louis Philippe. More than this, the generous king had Marigny's son sent to school in France, entirely at the expense of the French taxpayers.

But in 1800 when his father died Bernard Marigny was the richest fifteen-year-old lad in America. Uncle De Lino de Chalmette assumed management of the vast estate and guardianship of its heir. This latter proved an even vaster responsibility. Bernard was as willful and headstrong and wild as the coffee and cream colored waters of the Mississippi in flood stage, when they swirled past the great Marigny mansion on its bank just below the Esplanade. Chalmette shipped his charge off to London. This was supposed to do young Marigny a lot of good, not to mention De Lino de Chalmette.

Abroad the youth speedily learned what has since been described as his most notable contribution to the make-up of the "true Creole type"; namely, generous spending for pleasure, with haughty indifference to the cost. He also learned some English, with an accent which he never lost; and a game played with two dice, in which he seldom won. Marigny was back in New Orleans soon after Uncle Chalmette received the first shipload of bills. He brought the dice.

Now the mutual dislike of the Creoles and the Americans included name-calling. All Americans from the Mississippi-Ohio valley were called by the generic term, Kaintock. It didn't matter to the Creoles whether they came from Kentucky or not. Perhaps those who bragged the loudest in the harassing days of the Spaniards were Kentuckians. All the Creoles could remember were those startling revelations, roared at the top of a voice, as huge fists beat against a hairy chest, "I'm a chile of the snapping turtle! I was reared on panther milk, and I can lick my weight in wild cats. I'm half man, half alligator, I am— and I'm from Kaintock!"

This picturesque insistence upon being other parts of the animal kingdom in addition to the species homo was a quaint characteristic of the American frontiersman. The Creoles appear to have been convinced of the allegations however; and generations of Creole mothers frightened their children into good conduct by threatening to throw them to the ferocious Kaintocks, half-and-half men and alligators.

On the other hand, the Americans' derisive name for the Creoles was Johnny Crapaud. In itself, Johnny Crapaud was as innocuous as Kaintock. In French, crapaud means frog; and Englishmen had long called Frenchmen Johnny Crapauds, because Frenchmen ate frog legs. Like so many bitter denunciations, these two labels acquired a venom which in themselves they did not convey.

Today in New Orleans there is a Kentucky street; and there used to be a—but let Bernard Marigny's story explain that.

Upon his return with the two dice, he taught his Creole friends the intriguing game. When the Americans saw the frogs huddled around playing, they called it Johnny Crapaud's game. Later, when the Americans themselves took up the game it was with that name—crapaud. But the broad "a" pronunciation of the frontier soon pruned crapaud to craps; and craps it has remained.

Historians tell how everyone whom Marigny taught his game beat him playing it. And Marigny taught everybody in town. This along with other interesting ways of disposing of nearly a million dollars, in time reduced him to selling his real estate. Records indicate that this shortage of ready cash developed two years after Marigny became master of his fortune. Uncle Chalmette turned the books over to him on his eighteenth birthday; and in 1808, when he was twenty, he applied to the city council for permission to subdivide part of his plantation nearest the city into lots.

In the Faubourg Marigny, which resulted, Bernard named the streets. And one of them, on which he is said to have lost numerous lots playing his beloved game, he impishly labeled Craps! Strikingly is revealed the character of Bernard Marigny in the names he selected for the streets in this early suburb of New Orleans. His swaggering and domineering nature is there, and so are his ready wit and biting satire. Also in evidence are his poor business judgment and neglected education which, his contemporaries declare, contributed so much to his financial ruin.

Creole vs. Kaintock—Round Two

The width of a street which included a sawmill canal and two roadways insured its position as the main thoroughfare of the new Faubourg. Marigny named it the Champs Elysées—the Elysian Fields, or Elysium which Virgil describes as the deathless residence of the spirits of the blessed. There at the river end of the Elysian Fields lived Marigny! This is more classical association than Marigny was capable of. Once he confessed in the legislature, of which he was a member, that he failed to understand a charge against him couched in classical analogies. Most probably he named the street after the Champs Elysées in Paris, a comparison which so far has remained as remote as the mythological one.

Faubourg Marigny was separated from the city by the crumbling fortifications and commons beyond them. The upperline of the suburb was 100 French feet below present-day Esplanade avenue. Marigny's surveyor lined the streets up with the river and the sawmill canal which Peter Marigny had dug. Thus were all the streets in the faubourg at a 50 degree variance with the alignment of streets in Pauger's original city. In 1808, Faubourg Marigny was a separate community, with separate street names. On the upper side of Elysian Fields, Marigny named the streets Frenchmen, Union, Bagatelle, Antoine, and Annette. Two other streets, laid at the same triangulations as the streets of the Vieux Carré, and seemingly planned as hitching posts whenever the two sections joined, he called Peace and History streets.

In the chapter, "Growing Pains," it has already been explained how Marigny named a street Frenchmen, in recollection of Lafrenniere and his lieutenants who died there for liberty in 1768.

Union was named for the Federal Union. It has since been changed to Touro, for there already was a Union street in the Faubourg Ste. Marie. Bagatelle has also been changed; it is now Pauger street. Antoine recalls Marigny's son, Antoine James, better known as Mandeville Marigny.

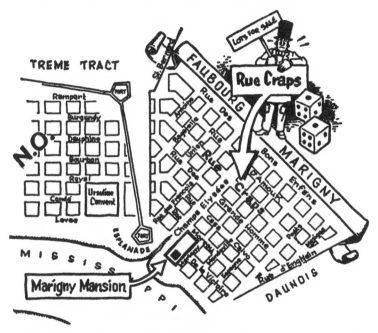

As for Annette street—Marigny's two wives were Mary Ann Jones and Anne Mathilde Morales. And Peace and History streets are now both called Kerlerec.

On the lower side of Elysian Fields are two streets bearing the two titular designations which this family of Philippe added to its patronymic—Marigny and Mandeville. Following them is the street called Spain. Two others Bernard Marigny labeled Poets and Music. Although he could not play, Marigny loved music. While in the legislature he did try to write some poetry, which was so bad it provoked a duel. A final street in the faubourg, its lowerline, was named for the Duke of Enghein, who was brutally executed by Napoleon who surmised that the Duke may have instigated a plot to assassinate him. As a street name, Enghein was popularly mispronounced "en-JINE." It was later changed to Lafayette, and then again to its present name of Almonester, which is officially misspelled Almonaster. Poets street was also changed; it is now called St. Roch.

The crossing streets in the faubourg, after Levee street which was on the river were: Victory, Moreau, Casa Calvo, Greatmen, Craps, Love and Good Children. To explain these names, and to isolate Craps street properly it is necessary to give the names also in their original French: *Rue de la Victoire, Rue Moreau, Rue Casa Calvo, Rue Des Grands Hommes, Rue de Craps, Rue d'Amour,* and finally *Rue Des Bon Enfants.*

Although most of Marigny's streets perpendicular with the river are retained in the street nomenclature as he named them, none of these crossing streets are—and it was all because of Craps street.

Let's begin at the beginning, which in New Orleans is always at the river front. The first street, called street of the Victory, was the street General Jackson marched up from his victory at Chalmette. His headquarters were, for a time, at the Marigny house. Houseguests, too, were the Napoleonic General Moreau; and Casa Calvo, the last Spanish governor of New Orleans. Marigny swaggered a little here, when he thus served reminders that he was host to the great.

There is some uncertainty about the next street, called Street of the Great Men. It could apply to the aforementioned greats whom he had put up, and also include Washington for whom the Public Place on this street is named. But there is a legend, which when considered with the character of Marigny, is not without credibility. A certain pedantic little Frenchman was forever bragging in the cafés of the great men he knew abroad; he was something of a nuisance, especially to Marigny who didn't like his preeminence thus challenged—Marigny who knew a king. This little man lived on the street Marigny labeled Greatmen, with satirical emphasis.

The next street is Craps. It is to be observed that while all the other streets were originally rendered in French, this street was Rue de Craps. Not *Crapaud,* for frog; it was Craps, for the game of dice! Craps, which contributed much to the financial ruin of Marigny, also ruined his picturesque street nomenclature. City Ordinance Number 395 of November 20, 1850 changed it to Burgundy street. This ordinance also changed seventy-five other street names in the city! Alas, one can never be sure where a crap game will end.

But it was a different New Orleans in 1850 than in the early years of that century, when a younger devil-may-care Bernard Marigny had named his streets. Now the Great Creole was an humble clerk in the office of Mortgages and Conveyances, and what remained of his vast estate was mortgaged to the hilt at the Citizens Bank. And Craps street was an important thoroughfare, with three churches on it.

Largely through the activity of the congregations of these three churches, the Second Methodist Church, St. Paul's Lutheran, and Sts. Peter and Paul Catholic Church, the petition was circulated and the city council acted. Now no fortifications separated Faubourg Marigny from the original city, and the two were linked together. So the street names of the Vieux Carré were continued into Marigny's old faubourg, and all the way down to the lower city limits of the present city.

It has never been recorded what, if anything, Bernard Marigny had to say in comment of Ordinance Number 395 which erased his street names. He could have laughed. Because this man had a true instinct for street names, and regardless of the ordinance, two generations of residents in the neighborhood continued to call the streets by their original names.

Perhaps even more objectionable than Craps was the street behind it called Love, when we consider the kind of love it extolled. It was a custom of young Creole gentlemen to acquire quadroon mistresses, and establish them in cottages back of the town. It was a custom of long standing, and many free women of color who had quadroon daughters carefully schooled them for such careers. These women, one quarter Negro and the rest white blood, are reputed to have been extremely handsome and desirable wenches. The cottages where this illicit love was domiciled were on the back streets—Burgundy and Rampart. And Marigny's street, which continued Rampart, he realistically titled Street of Love.

His last street was called Good Children. A likely translation of *Rue Des Bon Enfants* might be Street of the Good (or Happy) Childhood. It was near the edge of the swamp, where crawfishing and other adventurous sport would surely give many happy hours to little boys—if not to their mothers. Historians, however, take one look at the map, where this street is revealed around the corner from the

Street of Love, and raise historical eyebrows. Anyway, Good Children street is St. Claude now.

In about 1828, when Samuel J. Peters and James H. Caldwell were trying to do business with Bernard Marigny, that proud Creole was about midway between his seat at the festive board with King Louis Philippe and his stool in the office of Mortgages and Conveyances. He was already heavily in debt at the Citizens Bank, but still listed on the board of directors of that institution. Nevertheless, Peters' persuasion won out, and Marigny agreed to sell. Perhaps his pride was touched when he heard the exciting plans Caldwell had for the development of his faubourg. Magnificent hotels, theaters, gas works, docks, and cotton presses. Caldwell was one of the finest actors of his day. Undoubtedly under the spell of his eloquence Marigny could smell the gas works and hear chanting longshoremen along the docks. A day was set for the signing of all the papers before a notary.

But upon the appointed day, Madame Marigny could not be found. She had certain rights in the property to be transferred. Without her signature the deal could not be consummated. Where was she?

Peters suspected Marigny of trickery, of trying to wiggle out of his agreement. "How should I know where she is? I told her to come," shrugged Marigny. His insolence, which was characteristic, increased Peters' suspicions, whose patience was at last exhausted.

"Sir," he shouted at the Creole, "I shall live, by God, to see the day when rank grass will choke up the gutters of your old Faubourg!" And he stormed out.

From this meeting began Marigny's decline in political

prestige among the Creole element of the city. And across the commons, in the Faubourg Ste. Marie, his treatment of the Americans touched off fires of burning determination in the activities of Peters and Caldwell. They would outstrip the Creoles!

But perhaps Marigny's disappointment matched Peters'. For his wife was absent on her own accord. For some time she had been asking for restitution of her own paraphernal rights, but Marigny would never consent. Many times she threatened to get even with him for this. She did, and Faubourg Marigny lost its golden opportunity.

Later Marigny sought to match the American progress uptown. Relics of his futile effort are a Port street and a Cottonpress (now shortened to Press) street in this neighborhood. What once was Faubourg Marigny remains a sleepy and tired looking adjunct to the Vieux Carré, largely double tenement residential in character.

In 1835 the Americans were able to push through the legislature a new charter which divided the city into three municipalities. Canal street and Esplanade Avenue were the divisions of the First Municipality. The Second Municipality was the American Section above Canal street; and the Third were the Faubourgs of Marigny and Washington, further downriver.

Immediately property values in the American section rose, and things hummed. Streets were paved, wharves were built, hotels and theaters—daring in both size and elaborate design—rose from the "great quagmire," as the Creoles contemptuously termed Gravier's Faubourg Ste. Marie. Nor was this all. Churches, banks, and structures both commercial and residential appeared with magic swiftness. Even a City Hall appeared to rival the Cabildo!

Seventeen years later, when a reorganized government once more united the municipalities, the American section was secure as the commercial citadel of New Orleans. The Creoles had lost the second round, and with it ended the bitterly contested rivalry between the two factions. Now, only in smaller, trifling matters would the old animosity linger.

Not without its amusing feature was the violent Creole objection to the Act of the Legislature of 1899 creating the Sewerage and Water Board. A sewerage system was to be installed, and also a water purification plant. The Creoles suspected trickery. Sanitary toilets were to be ordered used, and they were going to make you buy water to flush them! To save the measure and appease the Creoles, the law was actually amended to provide free water for flushing toilets in New Orleans. To this day, one fourth of the total domestic consumption of water is provided free of cost to the consumer!

Yes, upon occasion, the Creoles could bounce back.

It is doubtful if, in the final analysis, they lost anything at all. Their quaint and obstinate ways, which first confused and then stimulated their first American associates into bustling activity, have now permeated the whole. Today, the distinguishing characteristic and charm of New Orleans are due to the imperishable influence of these children of the colonies—The Creoles.

It is strange that there is not, and never has been, a Creole street in New Orleans.

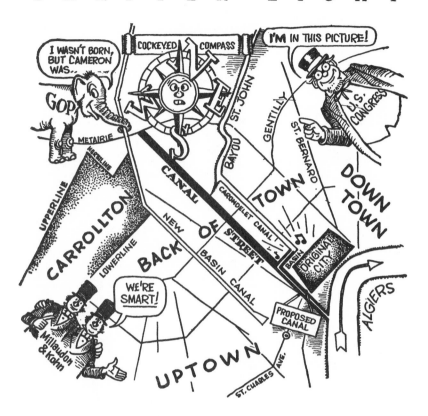

Canal Street –
and Contrasts

CANAL STREET —
AND CONTRASTS

"The claims of the corporation of the city of New Orleans, to the commons adjacent to the said city, and within six hundred yards from the fortifications of the same, are hereby recognized and confirmed . . . provided, that the corporation shall reserve for the purpose, and convey gratuitously for the public benefit, to the company authorized by the Legislature of the Territory of Louisiana, as much of the said commons as shall be necessary to continue the Canal of Carondelet from the present basin to the Mississippi, and shall not dispose of, for the purpose of building thereon, any lot within 60 feet of the space reserved for a canal, which shall forever remain open as a public highway . . ."

U. S. Statutes at large; Vol. 2; page 440; sec. 3.

*T*HE foregoing is from an Act of Congress, dated March 3, 1807. It explains how New Orleans' world famous boulevard acquired its extraordinary width, and its exceedingly ordinary name—Canal street.

From property line to property line Canal street is 171 feet wide; but fifty feet of this were reserved for a canal until 1852 by no less an authority than the Congress of the United States. That year the Orleans Navigation Company became insolvent, and its charter forfeited. Canal street was then legally entitled to remain a street 171 feet wide.

But even before the legality of its width was settled, Canal street gave great promise for the future. It began to achieve importance in the 1830's. One who contributed much to its growth was the merchant Judah Touro; and when he died in 1854 he actually remembered it in his will, bequeathing between two and three hundred thousand dollars for the beautification of his beloved street. In a spontaneous burst of appreciation, the city council passed an ordinance renaming this street, Touro Avenue. But it does not appear that anybody at all paid the slightest attention to this change; even in official documents the street continued to be called Canal. On May 19, 1855 the council met and quietly slid through another ordinance "that the name of Touro Avenue be and is hereby changed to the original name of Canal Street." The canal which gave the street its impressive breadth thus continued to bestow upon it its name—the canal that never was!

The Orleans Navigation Company, empowered by Congress to dig a canal on Canal street, has a curious place in New Orleans' history. The fact that it never dug the canal is strikingly symbolic of its life-long performance. It never did much of anything, save engage in endless squabbles with the city council. Of its president, Laurent Millaudon, it is said that his name appears in court records of the period with a frequency exceeded only by John McDonogh's.

The territorial legislature chartered the company in

1805, for the purpose of making the Carondelet Canal and Bayou St. John fit for navigation. This canal had been dug by the Spanish governor, Carondelet, and extended the bayou to the ramparts in the rear of the city. When the United States acquired Louisiana, Carondelet's canal was a neglected ditch of stagnant water, useless for either drainage or navigation.

In an initial spurt of energy the Orleans Navigation Company cleared and widened the canal, improved its turning basin, and dredged out Bayou St. John. A sum of $375,000 was spent on this work, and then the Navigation Company appears to have sat back for about forty years, collecting tolls from vessels which used the waterway, and speculating in real estate. The ambitious plans to extend the canal from its turning basin, along the street which acquired the name of Basin, to the street which acquired the name of Canal, and thence to the river, never came any closer to reality than a legendary legend on maps of New Orleans for a generation, reading "Proposed Route of Canal."

But real and lively have been the two streets named to mark its right-of-way. Lower Basin street, so called because it was on the lower side of Canal street, was the birthplace of jazz music, as the New Orleans Jazz Foundation is prepared to prove. It was also the "main street" of Storyville, New Orleans' one-time notorious red-light district, where in 1897 an effort was made geographically to limit the practice of prostitution.

Canal street, in New Orleans, is more than a street. It is a division separating uptown and downtown. From the river's batture to Rampart, no street name crosses its broad expanse; and nowhere along its three and a half mile length do house numbers cross it. Canal street and the river are the points of orientation for all house numbering in New Orleans, and houses on streets going uptown and downtown both begin with number 100 at Canal street.

Beyond Rampart, where the streets begin to cross Canal with the same name, they are prefixed North and South. It is not to be assumed that in New Orleans these prefixes have anything whatsoever to do with the compass. A North street simply means that it is downtown from Canal street, while a South street is on the other side, or uptown. To be sure, the streets downtown from Canal do run northeast for a dozen blocks. The unwary may be lured into the belief that if they persist along these streets their direction will improve in a more northerly manner. But the exact opposite is the case! All the North streets which reach St. Bernard Avenue turn there and continue due east; others nearest the river which achieve the greatest length, end their deceptive ways pointing southeast!

No more trustworthy are the uptown streets, prefixed South. South Claiborne, for instance, for three quarters of a mile of its length comes closer to running north than any of the downtown streets off of Canal which are labeled North!

Insofar as the other two points of the compass are concerned, the city has a West End Boulevard, and an Eastern Avenue. Both of these streets run north and south. West End Boulevard runs to West End, which is north of New Orleans on the western edge of its incorporated lakefront; Eastern Avenue was once the eastern street of the Gentilly Terrace subdivision, which the growing city has enveloped.

Canal street is entirely a product of the American domination in New Orleans. It was a nameless, no man's land between the crumbling fortifications of the Vieux Carré and the Faubourg Ste. Marie, when Claiborne arrived to be the first American governor. In 1806 a resolution of the city council declares that "the people had a right to complain that there is no other road between the city and the Faubourg than the Tchoupitoulas gate." The council further agreed that it was inconvenient. It is not immediately evident that the council did any more about it at the time.

The lower line of the Faubourg Ste. Marie was Common street, which was also the upperline of the commons. Between Rampart and the river the commons was a pie-shaped area, two blocks wide at Rampart (from Common to Iberville) and coming to a point at Common and Tchoupitoulas streets. Beyond Rampart it ranged behind the original city to the Carondelet Canal, and extended as far back as Claiborne. These are the boundaries on the official Sulakowski map, recognized by the United States Government.

Three years after the claims of the city of New Orleans to this commons were approved by Congress, the city purchased the plantation of Claude Treme, which lay between the Carondelet Canal and St. Bernard Avenue, also beyond Rampart and as far back as Claiborne. The price was $40,000. When it was divided into squares and lots, one of the streets was called for its former owner; and so St. Claude, major downtown boulevard, got its name.

As for Common street, all but seven blocks of its length was changed to Tulane Avenue in 1886. This was in appreciation of the generous bequest of the merchant, Paul Tulane, to the University of Louisiana, which was then located on Common and University Place. In this rechristening the city council was more successful; Common street beyond Rampart remained and is still called Tulane Avenue. However, eight years after this, the university which was renamed for Tulane as was Common street, moved sixty-eight blocks away from it all to the present location of Gibson Hall on St. Charles Avenue, opposite Audubon Park. It is only accidental that, years later, the Charity Hospital Medical Center was established on Tulane Avenue, and Tulane's famous medical school is included in the group.

In 1835, when the animosity of the Creoles and the Americans in the Faubourg Ste. Marie divided the city into separate municipalities, Canal street was in a strategic location. It was neutral territory!

Here enterprising merchants might establish and draw trade from both hostile—but well-heeled—camps. Judah Touro built his imposing "Touro Block" and found ready tenants. A. D. Crossman, who later became mayor, was among the first to locate on the broad street. Daniel Holmes was another; and his establishment, which developed into one of the first great American department stores, is still doing very well at its Canal street address. Joshua Baldwin, Edward York, James Breedlove, Peter Conery, Maunsell White, and the Frerets were other men of merchandise who pioneered on the street.

Canal street had its bonanza; and it has never ceased to enjoy this distinct characteristic which it first acquired when the city was torn asunder. It is still the mecca for shoppers in New Orleans! When Madame New Orleans lives downtown she goes *"up* to Canal street"; when uptown she goes *"down* to Canal street"; and when she lives in such newer, back-of-town subdivisions as Lakeview,

Metairie, and Gentilly—then her expression is that she is going "*in* to Canal street for some shopping."

Here also two languages met head on. The sales personnel of Canal street stores necessarily included French-speaking clerks for the downtown Creoles, and English speakers for the uptown customers. It was a bi-lingual trade, which, in 1837, prompted the Citizens Bank to print its ten-dollar bank-notes with one side English and the other French. The French side prominently displayed the French word for ten, DIX; and the best documented legend for the origin of DIXIE, the South's nickname, gives full credit to these bank-notes and the mispronunciation of their French side by Kentucky keelboatmen. Incidentally, in all Louisiana, French continued to be an official language along with English, requiring due publication of all official matters in both languages, until the constitutional convention of 1921.

New Orleans has always been, and still is, a city of canals, making it properly symbolic that the city's main street should be so named. Against Venice's 28 miles of canals, New Orleans in 1945 counted 108 miles! Neither does this include the city's Grand Canal—the Mississippi river. And for those who will say: "Yes, but in Venice there are nearly 90 miles more of watery alleys (or calli)." For those let it be known that besides New Orleans' 108 miles of canals, are 970 miles of subsurface arteries (many over a yard in diameter) for the drainage of its rainwater. Nearly 90 miles of New Orleans' canals are for this same system of drainage.

The city's navigable canals—the Industrial and Intracoastal—are important now as the old and new Basins were commercially valuable a hundred years ago. The Old Basin was the Bayou St. John-Carondelet Canal waterway, and the New Basin was dug by the Americans in 1832-38. For many years imports via these two canals totaled $1,500,000 per annum. As the channel of the New Basin canal was laboriously cut to the lake, a pattern of future growth for the city also resulted. The New Basin Canal was part of the Americans' plan to make themselves entirely self-sufficient from the Creoles. In 1832 an excavation such as this through a swamp bears mention in the same breath with the Panama Canal. The ditch was hacked out with pick and shovel, and countless cypress stumps likewise disposed of. There was no dynamite, nothing but wheelbarrows with which to haul the mud from the workings, and no other way to keep swamp seepage out save the back-breaking type of pump Archimedes had invented in 287 B. C.

Richard Delafield, of the U. S. Engineers, in analyzing the cost of the project, estimated that the canal, including jetties, wharves and trimmings, could be built for $217,-551. The cost proved to be five times that—even with labor at $20 a month, cost of housing and boarding men at $6.20 monthly, and lumber at $22 per thousand feet. Many German and Irish immigrants were imported for the work. There were frequent epidemics of cholera and yellow fever, until, in human life, the cost of the New Basin Canal has been placed at 8,000 souls.

In 1946 the city of New Orleans was authorized by a constitutional amendment to fill this canal up!

Even before ground was broken, the New Basin broke records. The establishment of the Canal Bank, for its financing, marked the first "improvement bank" in the city. Afterwards, in rapid succession other such banks sprang up to (1) build a gas works, (2) build the St. Charles

Hotel, (3) build the St. Louis Hotel, (4) the waterworks, and numerous railroad projects. And one of the organizers of the Republican Party bossed the digging operations.

In consideration for the Jeffersonian finer feelings of Orleanians then and now, it should be hastily added that the Republican Party did not happen until a few years after the canal was dug under the general managing of Simon Cameron. This most astute of American politicians did not become influential in the politics of his native Pennsylvania until 1845. After that he never ceased to be until his death in 1889. His prominence as a Republican resulted in his appointment to the important post of secretary of war in Lincoln's cabinet, charged with the prosecution of the war against the Southern Confederacy, which included New Orleans. Cameron's domination of Pennsylvania politics is one of the all-time classic examples of American boss rule. He was never beaten for office, and only retired when he had a son to occupy his seat in the U. S. Senate. To Simon Cameron is attributed that classic definition of an honest politician: "One who when he is bought will stay bought." Unknown to the Democratic National Committee, there is a Cameron street in modern New Orleans!

Among the real estate properties which the Canal Bank purchased for right-of-ways was a one half ownership in the Macarty Plantation for $130,000. The other half was owned jointly by Laurent Millaudon, Samuel Kohn, and John Slidell. These co-owners engaged the German surveyor, Charles Zimpel, to divide the land into squares and streets. This was in 1833, and twelve years later the subdivision was incorporated into the town of Carrollton.

How Carrollton got its name is a matter of some conjecture. While Charles Carroll of Carrollton may have been the inspiration for it, there is greater evidence that the community was named for William Carroll, general of militia and later governor of the state of Tennessee. General Carroll came with 2,500 men to join Jackson and defend New Orleans in 1815. He, and his army, camped on the Macarty Plantation, which later became Carrollton. In 1825, while serving his second term as Tennessee's governor, Carroll visited New Orleans, and there was a great reception in his honor.

Also, across Lake Pontchartrain Bernard Marigny had subdivided part of his estate into the village of Mandeville. There, among the streets, are two named Carroll and Coffee,—both generals at the Battle of New Orleans. Mandeville was laid out just three years before Carrollton.

There is a great deal more reason for a bunch of expert promoters, such as Millaudon, Kohn, et al, to name a new subdivision for a local hero, or at least, one who had become a hero locally. Here within the environs of the new subdivision, Carroll and his valiant Tennesseans had rested before going into the lines at Chalmette. It is the sort of appeal that could be whipped up to the point where a prospect would begin to doubt his patriotism if he didn't buy a lot in Carrollton. Especially, if he, the prospect, came to New Orleans from Tennessee; and many did. Carrollton was a successful land development from the start.

Just as there never was a canal on Canal street, between Rampart and the river, there never was a canal on Canal Avenue—main boulevard of the village of Carrollton. The street was simply named for the New Basin Canal. The continuation of Canal Avenue, beyond the New Basin, was first to be called Carrollton Avenue. Curiously, this was not within the corporate limits of Carrollton. The name was later made to apply to the street's entire length.

A great variety of street names in Carrollton have resulted from a great variety of namers. Zimpel laid out the town in huge 650-foot squares. Purchasers were permitted to make their own subdivision, but obliged by law to quarter each 650-foot square into four 300-footers, separated by 50-foot streets. Usually the first owners to subdivide named the new streets, and adjacent squares—when drawn and quartered later—adopted the already established names. Eagle, Dublin, and Belfast are among the earlier ones who got a two block start and grew into long streets.

Other Carrollton streets so conceived bear the names of pioneer villagers; such as Samuel Short, Charles Huso, and Solomon Cohn who established Carrollton's first industry, a rope walk. Until Civil War times, ropes were woven by hand not much differently than they had been from the beginning of recorded history. A rope walk was a long, alley-like shelter which housed the operation. Inside, the rope weaver, having drawn the proper number of fibers for the strand of rope yarn desired, fixed them to a wheel at one end of the walk. The wheel was turned by an assistant; and the weaver, with other fibers wrapped around his wrist, walked backward down the rope walk, feeding them into the twisting strand. Cording of the finished yarn into rope was done much the same way. Rope walks varied in length from a few hundred feet to almost a thousand, their length usually determined the length of rope which could be corded. Every coastal American community had its rope walk, and Carrollton had Cohn's.

The name of the village's promoter, Laurent Millaudon, is represented in the street nomenclature; and so is

John Green's, whose extensive uptown real estate invest-
ments included holdings in Carrollton. Charles Zimpel
seemingly liked his surveying well enough to buy some,
hence Zimpel street which has been misspelled into Zim-
ple. But various lawyers, city attorneys and engineers who
have struggled with an error of Zimpel's in running the
lower line of Carrollton would like to muss up this Prus-
sian even more. Zimpel spent his youth in the service of
Frederick William III.

The lower line (now Lowerline street) originally ran
straight back to Apricot street; there it jogged one short
square to the right and continued on to the New Basin
Canal. Here at Apricot is where Zimpel corrected the error
in his line; but not until recent years were conflicts in ownership finally settled. Today Pine street is continued from
Apricot on the line that Zimpel named Lowerline; and
Lowerline street beyond Apricot runs straight to the New
Basin Canal. Formerly, under Zimpel's plan, these last
twelve blocks of Lowerline were named Bernadotte street
—a street which Zimpel slipped in when he corrected his
lower line.

But before its demise, this extra street influenced the
street nomenclature in another Zimpel job on the other
side of the New Basin. (John Arrowsmith's Faubourg Jackson, told in a later chapter.) And it also appears suspi-
ciously evident that the Carrollton street named Burdette,
which at Forshey street laterals off of one-time Bernadotte
street, is a corruption of the street named for Napoleon's
general who got himself elected king of Sweden.

Originally, many Carrollton streets were named for
presidents, but because of duplications in other sections of
New Orleans, only Adams and Monroe remain. A street

named for Washington, for instance, was changed from the name of the first president to that of the first mayor of Carrollton, Hampton.

With the exception of Monticello, which was the upper line of Carrollton, and called Upperline, other boundaries of this former village are evident by such streets as Lowerline and Northline. Another street named Upperline, twenty-five blocks below Lowerline street is the upper line of the Bouligny plantation, with no relation to Carrollton except confusing similarity.

The road alongside the New Basin Canal, now Pontchartrain Boulevard but long known as the Shell Road, has always been part of Carrollton life. Until 1910 tolls were collected for use of this road to the lake, 6½¢ for a man on horseback and 25¢ for carriages.

Perhaps it is best that Carrollton's Canal Avenue was changed to Carrollton Avenue. Even for a city with more canals than Venice, and a nomenclature of streets with its Lowerlines above its Upperlines, to have a street corner be the intersection of Canal and Canal would be extreme. Especially when one Canal street was named for a canal that was never dug, and the other for a canal scheduled to be filled up.

The Americans
Had Class

THE AMERICANS
HAD CLASS

*I*N THE vernacular of sports writers, those men who built the American section of New Orleans had class! During the period from 1825 they overcame a hundred year lead of the Creoles, and scored lasting recollection for their section as the commercial district of the city.

There were many stellar performers. But perhaps a first string line-up would include Thomas Banks, builder of Banks Arcade where (among other things) the Texas Revolution was planned; R. C. Prichard, the hotel man; Maunsell White, capitalist, promoter, and originator of improvement banks; William Freret, whose immense cotton press sprawled over two squares between St. Charles and Baronne streets; Edward York, merchant and great advocate of public schools; A. D. Crossman, pioneer Canal street merchant, who like Freret later became mayor; James Breedlove, the banker; Peter Conery and Stephen (Old Moneybags) Henderson, merchants and industrialists; and two who sparked the team—Samuel J. Peters and James H. Caldwell.

Today, in New Orleans, streets bear the names of ten of

these All-American city builders; but for the eleventh man there is no street named Caldwell. Yet, he had more class than any of his team mates. James H. Caldwell had class in sports page patois, and he was an exceptional scholar of the classics.

Caldwell was an actor, whose own life was his greatest role. For forty years he and New Orleans co-starred in an extravaganza of make-believe so realistically played that, like Pygmalion's masterpiece, it lived. He dreamed great dreams, did Caldwell, and so furious was his energy, so relentless his driving force, so strong and steadfast his confidence in himself that he made those dreams come true.

In 1822 he blazed the trail for the Americans into the Faubourg Ste. Marie, when he broke ground for his American Theater on Camp street near Poydras. Writing twenty years later Caldwell's own words best describe this initial venture: "Such was the situation at that time, in what is now the Second Municipality, that the streets in which are some of the greatest monuments were scarcely even defined. New Levee street (now called Peters) was a continuous line of ponds for more than a mile, and Tchoupitoulas and Magazine could then boast of no better buildings than such as are denominated as shanties, with here and there the mouldering remains of a former plantation residence. Camp street had only at that time a few tobacco and cotton warehouses, and St. Charles street was best known to the boys, who sought in sport for snipe among the latanier in the marshes, which had never been disturbed otherwise in their original growth.

"The gradual rising of the walls of the first American Theatre excited a great deal of curiosity, and naturally so, for people conceived no merchantile use for such a building, speculated jocularly on the idea of its being intended for a fortification . . . For several years the people had to travel on gunwale sidewalks; and carriages could not be used after a heavy rain so far out of the way as Camp street . . . The success attendant on my building the American Theatre rendered it a nucleus around which may be said to have settled and called into existence the Second Municipality."

James H. Caldwell, obviously, was one who could blow his own horn. But he was exactly correct in declaring that this theater stimulated growth of the city above Canal street; and in the development that followed, Caldwell was ever in the vanguard. By 1835 he had built the St. Charles Theater, a playhouse whose lavishness was surpassed in all the world by only three others in Italy. His "Utopian ideas" accounted for the design and the completion of the first St. Charles Hotel, which rose from the pigsties and butterbean sections of Pierre Percy's truck garden to dominate the New Orleans skyline. This was in 1837, and departing guests passed through its Corinthian portico to spread its fame to the world. The St. Charles was the first of the great American hotels; the present hotel of that name occupies the same site.

Not the least of Caldwell's enterprises was the gas works. Single-handed, and with his own resources in the beginning, Caldwell placed New Orleans among the first four American cities lit by gas. He conceived the idea; journeyed to England to purchase the gas making machine; and personally superintended construction of the works back on Magnolia and Perdido streets. Then, to finance its continuance, he secured a charter for the New Orleans Gas Light and Banking Company with a capital stock of six million dollars. Some of the sturdy buildings Caldwell built in 1835 were still being used by the present New Orleans gas company in 1946. He also headed companies to install gas in the cities of Cincinnati and Mobile.

New Orleans benefited from this man's amazing energy and his great vision, but Caldwell was no benefactor to his contemporaries. He was a monopolist in all his enterprises. He resented competition and bashed it down whenever he could, particularly theatrical competition. The Cincinnati *Daily Gazette* of November 16, 1836 sums the man up thus: "Mr. Caldwell of New Orleans, not satisfied with owning all the theatres between the Falls of St. Anthony (Minneapolis) and the Balize (the mouth of the Mississippi), and managing two or three of them, with being the proprietor of a bank, and the largest bathing establishment in the Union—and with holding contracts for lighting three cities with gas, has a new project on foot—the foundation of the Ocean Steam Company for running a line of packets between New Orleans and Liverpool. While he is thinking about it, he is amusing himself with the scheme for paving the streets of New Orleans with octagonal blocks of stone."

And yet he was not wholly the promoter. Although he made a fortune from his gas enterprises, his heart was in the theater; and before the footlights Caldwell was the finest light comedian of his day. Rival actors conceded this, and, under his management, every great star of the English speaking stage performed in New Orleans.

His private life is obscure, but this is not nearly so strange as that he had any time for private life at all. There were at least two Mrs. Caldwells, and there was also Jane Placide. Descendants of Caldwell believe his first wife to have been Margaret Placide, an actress. But in Caldwell's first theatrical company to come to New Orleans there is listed only an Eliza Placide; Jane appeared the following year.

Jane Placide was the daughter of M. and Mme. Alexander Placide, who came to America in 1792. Monsieur was a tumbler and gymnast, and Madame was a singer—a curious but successful team, who finally settled in Charleston, South Carolina, where M. Placide became manager of the local theater. Their children, Caroline, Henry, Thomas, and Jane, all became celebrated performers, but there was none named Margaret or Eliza. Historians are very inconsistent about these Placides; one claims that Caroline became Mrs. Blake, while another insists it was Mrs. Waring. Jane Placide's relationship with Caldwell is also puzzling.

In 1816, twenty-three-year-old James H. Caldwell arrived in Charleston, South Carolina. Placide's theater had burned down, and apparently most of the talent was snuffed out with it, for an agent had been sent to England to recruit players of whom Caldwell was one. Then Jane was age twelve. The theaterless new Louisiana territory beckoned to Caldwell, and four years later he arrived in New Orleans by way of Nashville and Natchez. This same year Caldwell had a son born, named William Shakespere, and in 1820 Caldwell does not appear to have been married to anyone except the theater. Then Jane Placide was sixteen, and had not made her début—as an actress, anyway.

But from 1825 to 1836 Jane Placide was the popular star of Caldwell's New Orleans theaters. The celebrated Edwin Forrest fell in love with her. When he discovered that Caldwell was her lover, he dramatically challenged the actor-manager to a duel. Historians explain that Caldwell was too busy to comply with this invitation, and that frustrated

Forrest quit the company. There is scant record or evidence of Caldwell's passion for Jane; he filed her death notice when she died in 1835, and ordered inscribed on her tomb in Girod Cemetery the sentimental verse of Barry Cornwall:

> "There's not an hour
> Of the day or dreaming night but I
> am with thee;
> Etc. etc. etc."

It's difficult to believe that busy Mr. Caldwell had many hours to be with anybody, except in this spiritual fashion. However, two years after Jane's funeral, and at the customary intervals, three children were born to a certain Margaret Abrams. She died in 1857, and nine years later Caldwell legally adopted two surviving sons.

But between the death of Margaret Abrams and this adoption, Caldwell married Josephine Rowe—daughter of his leading lady at the St. Charles Theater. In this relationship, he was ten years older than his mother-in-law. Nevertheless, he survived this young wife by five years, dying in New York in 1863. Then the nation was locked in a bloody civil war, but a way was found to transport the mortal remains of this fantastic man back to the city that was so largely of his building. He lies today in the "Family Tomb of James H. Caldwell," Lot E, Cypress Grove Cemetery.

. . . but for this eleventh man there is no street named Caldwell.

On the other hand, there has never been a lack of streets named for the tenth man in the line-up. There is North

Peters, South Peters, and there used to be a Peters Avenue. There is even St. Peter street! Also, Samuel J. Peters is called the Father of the Second Municipality.

Historians aptly describe this division of New Orleans into three municipalities as a "curious experiment in city affairs." It was actually a compromise attained by Peters. Most of his American associates wanted to incorporate the Faubourg Ste. Marie into an entirely separate city, just as the village of Lafayette above Felicity street had been in 1833. But the charter of 1836, sponsored by Peters, divided the one city into three separate corporations with three city councils and one mayor. The mayor, it was stipulated, must be over thirty, and own at least $5,000 in city property. Whether or not he could read and write appears to have been optional.

A modern relic of this divided municipal government is the badge now worn by New Orleans policemen—a star within a crescent. When it was adopted, some insignia was sought that symbolized all three of the municipalities; so the mayor's seal was chosen. And a symbol is all the mayor was during the seventeen years of the divided government. The real mayors were the three recorders of each municipality; and James H. Caldwell found time to be recorder of the Second Municipality for a term.

How reasonable it would be to declare that Caldwell fastened the many classical names to the suburban streets of the Second Municipality. Who else but one schooled in the whimsical nonsense of mythology and the Age of Fable would propose the name of Dryades for a street on the woods side of town, and Nayades for one nearer the river? Who but one well acquainted with the classics would recall that the Dryades were the wood nymphs, fragile girl

friends of Pan who are said to perish when their trees are
cut down. How aptly the name emphasized the persistent
urging of the city council that citizens plant trees, thus to
detract from the barrenness of the city area—and provide
an abode for the Dryades too! Incidentally, both Caldwell
and Pan would be no little surprised at the dusky nymphs
who now people the neighborhood of downtown Dryades
street, perched not on trees but on the wooden steps before
their shotgun houses. The section has become a Negro
neighborhood.

Lee Circle was called Tivoli Place, until Lee's monument was raised there in 1876. And how classically appropriate it was to have the name of Triton Walk for a broad
avenue leading from the street of the river nymphs to the
turning basin of the New Canal. Triton was the son of
Neptune and Amphitrite; he was sort of half man and half
fish, or a merman. In the 1830's countless barges were
daily unloading shells at the Covington and Amite Landings on the New Canal, shells with which the Americans
were mixing their cement, building their city.

On the other side of Tivoli Place this street was called
Delord; named for Delord Sarpy, whose plantation this
was. In 1889 Miss Annie T. Howard endowed a library on
Delord Street, and the name of both it and Triton Walk
became Howard Avenue. Now, although the Howard
Memorial Library has moved miles away to the campus of
Tulane University, the street continues to be called
Howard.

It would indeed be reasonable to conclude that Caldwell contributed the classical flavor to New Orleans street
nomenclature, and some historians generously so credit
him. But, alas, the classical names—which were first fas-

tened on the streets bounded by Howard, Felicity, Camp, and S. Rampart—appear on maps ten years before Caldwell came to town. It is only coincidental that this classical scholar and these classical street names happened so closely together.

Along with the Faubourg Ste. Marie, the Faubourgs Delord, Soulet, La Course, and Annunciation comprised the Second Municipality; and they extended, in that order from midway between St. Joseph street and Howard up to Felicity street. Between the years 1806-10, Barthelemy Lafon subdivided all four plantations. He made a single unit of the various properties, meticulously aligning the streets with those in the older Faubourg Ste. Marie.

Whatever else may be said of Lafon, he was a competent surveyor. Back of the line of Camp street, he displayed commendable cognizance of future growth when he swung the streets which parallel the river to commence a smaller arc within the great arc of the river between present-day Canal street and Carrollton Avenue. It is a pattern which was followed in the subdivision of the whole uptown.

Lafon gives every evidence of acting in an official capacity in designing this neighborhood. He was city surveyor then, and the territorial council had just created the College of Orleans. It occupied the site of the present St. Augustine Church on St. Claude and Gov. Nicholls streets. This college was part of an attempt of the government to create an educational system for Louisiana, and Lafon's subdivision appears to have been part of that project. The College of Orleans was an institution where one's education was measured with the lines of his translations from Homer and Plato, where the deans were affectionately called Titus and Tyrtaeus, where the air was heavy with Greek and Roman quotations. This educational system was to include preparatory school and public libraries throughout the territory.

Now, in the light of this, consider Lafon's plan back of Camp street. These streets wheeled around on a circle, called Tivoli Place; and one block beyond this circle, Camp street widened into a parkway named *Rue du Colisée.* Four blocks further along was a semi-circle (reserved for a basin or fountain), which supplemented Tivoli Place in wheeling the street plan. At this Basin the equally wide *Cours du Colisée* forked off the *Rue du Colisée;* and the triangular plot at this fork was actually reserved for a Coliseum! A third wide street led from the Basin to the *Prytanée,* one block back on a street called *Rue du Prytanée.* Today only along *Rue du Prytanée* are there nine crossing streets named for all the nine muses.

Here was the theme of the suburb. In ancient Greece, each village had its Prytaneum, dedicated to Hestia, goddess of the hearth. It functioned as the hearth of the community; there was kept the sacred fire; there was the religious and political center of the village; distinguished ambassadors, envoys and other visiting firemen were received by the city fathers at the Prytaneum, and quartered there for the duration of their visits. As time went on, the Prytaneum developed many other functions, even to the point, in Roman times, of becoming a hall of justice for trying murderers who could not be caught!

Later, as the French Revolution climbed out of its initial anarchy, the classic way of doing things, as opposed to the Bourbon monarchy, became the vogue. The French Revolution was nourished on Roman history which in turn had been well fed on Greek history. In France, the *Prytanée* evolved into a preparatory school—and that is what Lafon reserved for the two squares bounded by present-day Prytania, Euterpe, St. Charles, and Melpomene streets. The *Prytanée* was never built, but in some curious and obscure way twenty feet around these two blocks were dedicated to the United States government for a parade ground. Nobody knows by what title the government may claim this land, so the government doesn't, and the city of New Orleans assumes it is city property. Meanwhile, private property on these two blocks commences twenty feet back from the line of every other block in the neighborhood, and an ownerless strip of land serves to recall the *Prytanée* that has contributed Prytania street to the nomenclature.

Nor was the Coliseum ever built on its site bounded by present-day Camp, Race, Coliseum, and Euterpe streets. In Lafon's plan, the crossing streets were named for the muses only from Camp street back; on the river side of Camp each had a different name, until, in 1852, each street's full length was given the same name, and whenever it continued one of the muses' streets, that name prevailed.

New Orleans' Coliseum was not to have been one like the Romans had, where gladiators fought and Christians were fed to lions. Rather it was to be like the one in Paris; *Le Colisée de Paris* was principally a dance hall for the middle classes. It was built in 1771 at a cost of two million francs, then torn down seven years later for lack of patronage. Streets in Paris were cut through the site, notably one called *Rue du Colisée*. Apparently, the chief difference between the Coliseum street of New Orleans and that of Paris is that in New Orleans the street is named for a Coliseum that never had to be torn down because it was never built.

Mention must be made of Lafon's important street which ran out from the Tivoli Place, called *Cours du Nayades,* later Route of the Nayades, and now St. Charles Avenue. Curving through the uptown to Carrollton, this street imitates the great curve of the river as though guided by the river nymphs for whom it was originally called. And back of Nayades, only Dryades remains of Lafon's nomenclature. Apollo, Bacchus, and Hercules have become Carondelet, Baronne and Rampart; streets in the Faubourg Ste. Marie which they continue.

On the river side of Camp street, Lafon's plan and the street names show more consideration for the owners of these properties: Delord Sarpy, Thomas Soulet, Robin Delogny, and Jacques Livaudais. Some of these original names remain, such as, St. Thomas for Thomas Soulet; Celeste and St. James, for Celeste Marigny and her husband Jacques (James) Livaudais; and Constance, for the wife of Robin Delogny. Although there is still a Robin Street Wharf on the river, the street named Robin was one of those changed in 1852; it is now Euterpe.

Also, there were lesser landowners, who owned parts of the main tracts: such as Richard, Gaiennie, and Poeyfarre, whose names still remain as street names. Remaining, too, is a street called Market, which led to the Market which was never built; and Orange, because it ran through the orange grove which the Jesuit fathers planted when once this region was part of their vast plantation. Annunciation street gets its name from Livaudais' part of the subdivision, Faubourg Annunciation; and Robin Delogny called his tract, Faubourg De La Course—or Race Track. A street called La Course is now Race street.

Perhaps in 1806, when Delogny's faubourg was subdivided, there was a race track nearby. Many Creoles had race tracks on their plantations. It must be recognized, too, that when Lafon made the survey of these lands, they were even more wild and unsettled than was the Faubourg Ste. Marie as Caldwell described it when he built his American Theater. Also three important events occurred between the time of the survey and the time when the region became a settled neighborhood.

Napoleon, whose government made education a state monopoly, met his Waterloo. The territorial government of Louisiana was strongly influenced by Napoleonic France in planning its educational system. Joseph Lakanal, who had been chairman of education during the French Revolution, and who had remained prominent in French education during the Empire, came to New Orleans after Napoleon's fall. He was the last president of the College of Orleans.

The other two events were the admission of Louisiana to the Union, and the War of 1812, with the local preoccupation of the Battle of New Orleans. Following this war, the rapid growth of New Orleans was slowed; and when it resumed, the direction was different from the old Creole-dominated territorial set-up. The College of Orleans closed its doors, and the *Prytanée* and *Colisée* were forgotten. All that survived of the ambitious plans of Lafon and the territorial council were the classical names of the streets. These the Americans retained, because then it was the style in America to be classical.

This was the period of Greek Revival in the United

States, a phenomenal new interest in Ancient Greece which prevailed during the years 1820-50. It was principally expressed in the architecture of the period—although such American cities as Athens, Georgia; Troy and Ithaca, New York; and Sparta, in eleven states, owe their names to the enthusiasm of the time. The national capitol at Washington got its Grecian character because it was built in 1827; and most all of the important buildings in the Second Municipality of New Orleans were designed in the Greek manner. The City Hall, from the drawing board of James Gallier, is authoritatively called "one of the most beautiful examples of small Greek Revival public buildings to be found anywhere." The Marble Hall of the Custom House is another notable relic of the period, and there are many others.

It is readily seen how the Americans, who were enthusiastic about all things classical, found these classically named streets of Lafon's acceptable. All that remains of the Creoles' part in bestowing them is their pronunciation. To the consternation of most visitors, the streets named for the nine muses are still pronounced in a corruption of the French pronunciation.

In 1834, when activity in the American Section was at its height, John Gravier died at the age of 94. Henry Castellanos tells the pathetic story of this man who once owned all the area which the Americans made the heart of commercial New Orleans. In striving to compete with the enterprising, speculating newcomers, this old Creole not only lost his wealth and his property, but seemingly his reason also. Castellanos describes his last abode as ". . . an old shanty surrounded by weeping willows, amidst the ghastly scenes of a Louisiana swamp. No ordinary courage was required to venture alone within the precincts of that forbidding and desolate place. The dismal willows could be heard uttering plaintive sounds with every gust of wind. The remote spot was invested with the glamour of romance and associated with the scene of foul deeds. It was looked upon by the community as unhallowed ground. long shunned for residential purposes . . . today the name of Willow street recalls this section of New Orleans which citizens for so long called 'the quarter of the damned.' "

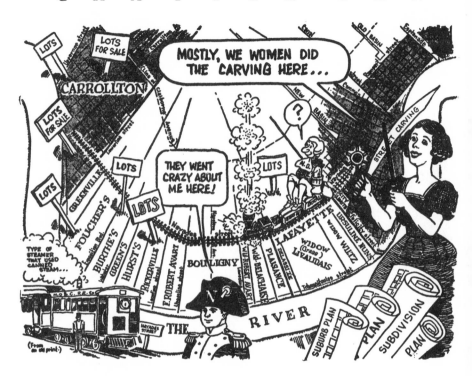

All Aboard for
Uptown

ALL ABOARD

FOR UPTOWN

SOON after the speculating Americans settled in the Faubourg Ste. Marie, calculating eyes were attracted to the region upriver from the Felicity street city limits. Beyond, fifteen plantations lined the riverbank, all the way up to the lower line of the Macarty tract, which soon became Lowerline street of Carrollton. These plantations now comprise the uptown section of New Orleans.

Originally, the uptown, along with the Faubourg Ste. Marie and Carrollton, formed the Chapitoulas Concession of Bienville. The ancient Road of the Chapitoulas became the Royal Road in colonial times, giving all the plantations communication with New Orleans. Now it is Tchoupitoulas street, and as late as Civil War times, the riverfront of the uptown was called the Tchoupitoulas Coast. But it was not along Tchoupitoulas street that New Orleans grew uptown.

It was hauled up there by a railroad!

In 1833, and a dozen years before the incorporation of Carrollton, the New Orleans & Carrollton Railroad was chartered. Beginning at Baronne and Poydras, the line ran up to the present intersection of St. Charles and Carrollton Avenues on precisely the same right-of-way now followed by the streetcars. Along this railroad track New Orleans commenced to grow uptown in 1835.

Service started September 25, of that year. The distance was 5.2 miles; the speed of the trains was four miles an hour. Slow? In a single lusty generation it transformed a rural countryside into the premier residential neighborhood of New Orleans.

Meanwhile, Lafayette was there to meet the first train. The same legislature which authorized the railroad acted to incorporate the village of Lafayette, adjacent to New Orleans just above Felicity street. The new village speedily became a haven for harassed Americans, who were still being outvoted and frustrated by Creole majorities in the city council. New Orleans had not yet been trisected into separate municipalities in 1833. So to Lafayette Americans flocked, and there many built the palatial mansions on spacious grounds which today characterize this neighborhood, popularly called the Garden District.

Numbered streets—from First to Ninth, but with no Fifth—almost count out Lafayette's street nomenclature as a storyteller. But other streets are more revealing. They tell of the three plantations from which Lafayette was formed, and of several women who pioneered the subdivision of the Uptown.

First above the city limits of New Orleans came three streets named Felicity, St. Mary and St. Andrew. These resulted from a sketchy subdivision of the Faubourg Des Religieuses, made in 1810 by Lafon. Presumedly, the Ursulines bought this land from Jacques Livaudais for a new convent site; but something, perhaps the close proximity of all the mythological, pagan names next door, caused a change of plan. The subdivision was made for more profitable disposition of the property, and the three streets which resulted were named for Sister Ste. Marie Oliviere, Mother Superior of the Ursuline convent; Sister Ste. Félicitée Alzac, her assistant; and Sister Ste. André Madiere, Depositaire of the convent. A careless map-maker once omitted the prefix of "saint" before Félicitée, and the error has never been corrected. Two other streets near the river, called Nuns and Religious, further identify the Ursulines with this neighborhood.

Margarethe Wiltz, under whose direction the next five blocks of Lafayette (measuring on Tchoupitoulas street) were subdivided, was the widow of Joseph Milhet, one of the patriots shot after the revolt of 1768; and Jacinto Panis, believed to have been the captain in charge of the Spanish firing squad.

Panis was also dead in 1824, when the Widow Wiltz (as she was called for convenience) began subdividing. For her second husband, she named the widest street Grand Route Panis. She named another street Rousseau, for Pierre George Rousseau who married her daughter Catherine Milhet, and a third she called Soraparu. Historians explain that Jean Baptiste Soraparu was just a friend of the family, but this isn't much of an explanation.

Three quarters of a mile up the river was the plantation of the widow's brother, Joseph Wiltz, who had an uncountable number of married grandchildren in 1824. So it is difficult to determine who in New Orleans was not related to the widow when she was naming streets, two others of which are called Josephine and Adele. It seems most likely that one of these is named for four-year-old Marie Josephine, daughter of Annette Wiltz and Edmund Valcourt. As for Adele, it was the No. 1 favorite name for Creoles of the feminine gender. It would be ridiculous if there was not among the uncountable Wiltzes one named Adele!

Recently, heated efforts have been made to prove that Adele street was the original Irish Channel, a sobriquet that drapes loosely over this whole neighborhood, because in the 1830's many Irish immigrants settled there. That Adele street is any more or less the Irish Channel than the next block, or around the corner, is a matter best left to Irishmen and historians for final settlement.

When the Widow Wiltz died, her daughter Catherine, who was then the Widow Rousseau, disposed of the property. It was under the ownership of Harrod & Ogdon, a brokerage firm, that its development continued. Harrod & Ogdon changed the name of Grand Route Panis to Jackson Avenue, and formally titled the whole subdivision, Faubourg Lafayette. Generals Jackson and Lafayette had been recent visitors to New Orleans.

A remnant of the great Livaudais plantation, which once extended from Euterpe street to Toledano, adjoined Faubourg Lafayette. Here again a widow was the owner, but Celeste Philippe Marigny Livaudais was a grass widow.

When this sister of Bernard Marigny married Jacques Livaudais, it was a union of the city's two greatest estates. But for the happiness of Celeste and Jacques, all their families' vast acres ever amounted to were grounds for divorce. In 1826, Celeste sued for separate bed and board; Jacques failing to appear in court, she became owner of the Livaudais plantation by default. Then she sailed for France, establishing an exceedingly separated bed and board from Jacques in a French chateau. There she acquired the title of Marquise, and lived like a Marquise—especially after the year 1832, when a syndicate of Americans paid her half a million dollars for the Livaudais plantation. This syndicate joined its holdings with Harrod & Ogdon's, acquired control of the Ursulines' faubourg, and had the whole incorporated into the village of Lafayette on April 1, 1833.

Philip street is named for Celeste Philippe Marigny Livaudais. It is several miles long. Livaudais street, near the riverfront, is one block long. It is named for Jacques, who certainly got the short end of the story of Lafayette in more ways than one.

Now follow twelve other plantations strung along the railroad track, between Lafayette and Carrollton. Each in its turn was figuratively jolted from sleepy rural isolation, and coupled with its neighbors, until all were joined together to form the uptown. In every case, names of the crossing streets identify and tell stories about the men and women who owned these lands.

Delassize and Plaisance go hand in hand . . .

Faubourg Delassize adjoined Livaudais' plantation. Valery Delassize purchased this three arpent frontage on the river from Jacques Livaudais, and operated a sawmill prior to the municipal history of Lafayette. But he was dead, and Samuel Herman was the owner who had it subdivided in 1836. Its two crossing streets were named Augustine and Eulalie. Eight years later, when the faubourg was annexed to Lafayette, the two streets were renamed Pleasant and Harmony.

Flanking Delassize on the uptown side was the four

arpent tract of Joseph Wiltz, which was subdivided in 1807 and called Quartier Plaisance. It was named for a community in Santo Domingo, from whence Jean Francois Ballon des Ravienes had come, Jean Francois who was the husband of granddaughter Marie Constance Wiltz. A canal separated Quartier Plaisance from Delassize, and near it Christoval Toledano bought land from Wiltz. The canal, and the roadway on its bank, came to be called Toledano.

Wiltz's suburb was a simple division into forty-two lots, with a wide street in the center, which he named Grand Route Wiltz. He dedicated all of his waterfront to public use, a benevolence which resulted in spirited legal wrangling after his death, when his numerous heirs tried to reclaim this valuable land. Considering such discord, it seems unlikely that Harmony crossed over the Toledano canal, as did Plaisance, to become a street name in Delassize. Grand Route Wiltz has been changed to Louisiana Avenue.

Mesdames Delachaise and Avart were widows too . . .
Auguste Delachaise inherited the Faubourg Delachaise from his grandfather, the unpopular Jacques, who had been sent to Louisiana after the fall of John Law. His job was to inquire into the condition of the colony. This he did courageously if not unwisely, and he made enemies. His death in 1730 was judged much too sudden to be natural. His wife who accompanied him to New Orleans, and survived him, is remembered for her quaint insistence that she was related to Joan of Arc. Historians neglect either to confirm or deny this. Jacques' uncle in France was a priest, the hard-working father confessor of Louis XIV.

Grandson Auguste made himself unpopular with Governor Carondelet, by trying to import the French Revolution and run the Spaniards out of Louisiana. Later, in 1803, he was killed in the Santo Domingo insurrection fighting another lost cause. So it was his widow—Marie Antoine Foucher Delachaise, a granddaughter of Etienne Boré—who subdivided Faubourg Delachaise and named four uptown streets. One she called Delachaise for her husband; another Aline for her daughter; and Antonine and Foucher for herself.

Next door, in the Faubourg St. Joseph, another widow subdivided her plantation. Madame Louis Robert Avart had no children, but Amelia Duplantier was her ward. She named a street for Amelia, and another for Dr. Tom Peniston whom Amelia married.

They loved Napoleon in Bouligny . . .

The New Orleans and Carrollton Railroad had a halfway stop on its 5.2 miles trek to Carrollton. Much about this railroad is interesting: it is reputed to have been the third oldest railroad in the United States; it was first to use "canned steam." The steam was made at each terminal and pumped into the "steamers," which quietly and sootlessly pulled their cars back and forth. The railroad's halfway stop is not without interest either.

For some mechanical reason peculiar to trains of the 1830's, this stop on the plantation of Louis Bouligny was necessary and prolonged. Laurent Millaudon and Samuel Kohn, promoters of Carrollton and board members of the railroad, hurriedly acquired a half interest in Faubourg Bouligny in 1834—while the railroad was under construction—and rushed in surveyor Zimpel to subdivide it.

These promoters were not the kind to let any prospects on the way to Carrollton get away at any halfway point. If the trains had to schedule a stop in Bouligny, they would have choice sites in uptown real estate there too, so Millaudon and Kohn must have reasoned.

Anyway, Faubourg Bouligny became a major promotion. It comprised the area between General Taylor and Upperline streets, and Zimpel's plan only extended back twelve blocks beyond St. Charles—then called Nayades street. Upperline was simply the upper line of the suburb; and the original name of General Taylor was Lowerline, for that is what it was.

At this time New Orleans was experiencing what has been called a great "French craze." Louis Philippe, Duke of Orleans, had been crowned king of France. Just ten years earlier the exiled Emperor Napoleon had died on St. Helena. Aware of the strength of the Bonapartists, the new king ordered Napoleon's statue replaced on the Place Vendome in Paris. French New Orleans felt itself much a part of all these momentous events. After all, the city had been named for the new king's great-great-grandfather, and, when in exile, Louis Philippe himself had visited New Orleans. (And borrowed money too.) As for Napoleon, his popularity had always been great. Only the Emperor's death had halted the ambitious plan of Nicholas Girod and Dominique You to move against the British fleet and rescue him from St. Helena.

And, this very year, 1834, Dr. Francesco Antommarchi, who had attended Napoleon in exile, arrived and opened an office on Royal street. A bronze death mask of Napoleon was presented to the city by the doctor. It is still to be seen in the Cabildo Museum. Yes, in 1834, the excitement and enthusiasm of New Orleans for things French and things Napoleonic were understandable.

It is therefore understandable why smart promoters like Millaudon and Kohn named the main street in their new suburb Napoleon Avenue. Other streets were called for great Napoleonic victories; Milan, Austerlitz, Berlin, Marengo, and Constantinople. Amid confused flushes of patriotism, Berlin street was changed to General Pershing during World War I. Young Napoleon first joined his regiment at Valence, so a street was called Valence. Lyon and Bordeaux are two French cities prominently identified with the Emperor's career. Why another street is named Cadiz is curiously out of line with the general complimentary treatment being accorded Napoleon. Cadiz, on the coast of southern Spain, was near enough to the Battle of Trafalgar for the guns to be heard. At Trafalgar Napoleon came in second best to Lord Nelson.*

After the fashion of signatures, two public places in Faubourg Bouligny were named Lawrence Square and Samuel Square, for Laurent (Lawrence) Millaudon and Samuel Kohn.

Almaris had a dowry . . .

In many ways, women's names and women namers feature the story of the uptown streets, but Almaris Robert Avart makes the most unique contribution to the story. Her father, Francois Robert Avart owned the plantation just above Bouligny, which he subdivided in 1841. He named one street Robert for himself, and three others for

---

* Some historians credit the Napoleonic names to Pierre Benjamin Buisson. This former lieutenant in the French Army settled in New Orleans after Waterloo, and was for some years official surveyor for Jefferson Parish and the Village of Lafayette.

Valmont Soniat Dufossat, the man who married Almaris. Another short street in the suburb he called Bellecastle, for a branch of the Soniat family which never migrated to America. A most unusual dowry!

The bank was stuck with Rickerville . . .

At the time of its subdivision in 1849, the City Bank owned five tenths of the plantation above Francois Robert Avart's. Along with others, Leontine Ricker and Octavia Ricker each owned a one tenth interest, which was enough to get streets named for them. The wide street was named for Samuel J. Peters, president of the City Bank. Later, Peters was changed to Jefferson.

Mr. Hurst's trains never came . . .

The uptown section from Joseph street to the lower line of Carrollton (Lowerline street) was the colonial plantations of Etienne Boré and his son-in-law, Pierre Foucher. It was here, in 1795, that these two first succeeded in producing granulated sugar in commercial quantities. That the football stadium of Tulane University, where the Sugar Bowl football game is played each New Year's Day, is located in this area is pleasingly appropriate. But in the 1830's, the first three blocks above Rickerville were owned by Cornelius Hurst.

When Hurst subdivided this property, which he called Hurstville, he named streets for his wife, Eleanor Smith, and for their children, who were Arabella and Joseph. Another street he called Hurst; and a fifth, which he called Nashville, he expected to put the whole family on easy street.

At this time James H. Caldwell was promoting a railroad to run from New Orleans to Nashville. Hurst sought to get a terminal, or spur, of the line to run into his sub-division, and in anticipation of the success of his scheme, he named his main street Nashville Avenue. However, the New Orleans and Nashville railroad never reached Nash-ville, or Hurstville either. It went broke in the Panic of 1837, and so did Cornelius Hurst.

Calhoun, Webster, and Clay were buried in style . . .
John Green owned a small subdivision above Hurst-ville, which was called Bloomingdale. Without much cere-mony, Green gave to the single street in his subdivision the name of State.

But next door, in Burtheville, Dominique Francois Burthe named the streets Webster, Henry Clay and Cal-houn, and these selections recall the momentous cere-monies which took place in New Orleans on December 9, 1852. It all began when the city learned of the death of Daniel Webster. A day of mourning was to be set aside for the great man. Then the city fathers remembered to their dismay that nothing had been done about Henry Clay who had died earlier that same year. Nor had fitting tribute been paid John Calhoun who had been dead two years. So funeral ceremonies in honor of all three were decided upon! Committees were hurriedly appointed and all or-ganizations in the city were invited to participate. Judge Burthe had a prominent post in the committee of arrange-ments.

December 9, 1852 dawned. It had rained the night be-fore. (It would in New Orleans.) But even so workmen had completed the huge Cenotaph in Lafayette Square. The procession, headed by a Grand Marshal and ending with the Association of Stevedores mounted on horses, was one and a half miles long, took an hour and forty minutes to pass a given point. It included such organizations as the Sons of Temperance, Screwmen's Benevolent Society, Mechanics Society, Typographical Union, Odd Fellows, and many others. But the funeral car was the feature of the column.

Designers of the funeral car were highly complimented by contemporary journals for their lavishness if not for their taste. It measured eleven feet long by eight wide, and towered sixteen feet. The bed or platform was a huge shell covered with black velvet, adorned with silver trimmings. Three huge bronze empty urns, one for each and bearing the names of the illustrious dead—Calhoun, Clay and Webster—in silver letters, stood in the center. Over it all was a great canopy of more black velvet with more silver trimmings. There was also gold and silver lace "in appropriate places." And above the canopy were perched two bronze screaming eagles. There was also a generous sized U. S. coat of arms somewhere on the car where there weren't any silver trimmings. The vehicle was drawn by six gray horses whose black velvet coverings were studded with silver stars and stamped with the shields of Massachusetts, South Carolina, and Kentucky. Each horse was led by a Negro groom, also draped in black velvet.

The procession began at City Hall. It went down St. Charles to Poydras, in Poydras to Tchoupitoulas, down Tchoupitoulas, across Canal then down North Peters to Toulouse, out Toulouse to Chartres, down Chartres to St. Ann, out St. Ann to Royal, up Royal to St. Louis, out St.

Louis to Bourbon, up Bourbon and across Canal again to Carondelet and thence to St. Joseph, in St. Joseph to Camp, then down Camp to Lafayette Square. Fortunately for the six horses and six Negroes bundled in black velvet, this was December.

In Lafayette Square the three bronze urns, inscribed with Calhoun, Clay, and Webster, were reverently removed from the funeral car and deposited in the Cenotaph. The ceremonies were concluded by long and eloquent eulogies, which—it has been reported—were "heard by large and evidently interested crowds."

On this day practically everybody in New Orleans was either in this funeral procession or witness to it. The only ones conspicuous by their absence were the three deceased who had already been buried in their own communities.

Exposition Boulevard follows Webster, Henry Clay, and Calhoun streets. Its name forever recalls the Cotton Centennial Exposition, held in Audubon Park in 1884-85. Although the city had purchased 12½ arpents of the old Foucher plantation in 1871 for $180,000, little effort was made to make it parklike until after this exposition which celebrated the 100th anniversary of the cotton gin.

The Uptown ended in Green's pastures . . .

Last of the uptown subdivisions was Greenville, which John Green was active in promoting. Not only was the suburb named for him; but every one of the four streets was called for green trees—Walnut, Chestnut, Magnolia, and Pine. Because other streets in the city had prior claims to the names of Chestnut and Magnolia, these two have been changed to Audubon and Broadway; but Walnut and

Pine remain as first inscribed in John Green's pastures. Above Pine street we cross Lowerline and enter Carrollton. This was the destination of the New Orleans & Carrollton Railroad.

And this is the way it hauled New Orleans uptown.

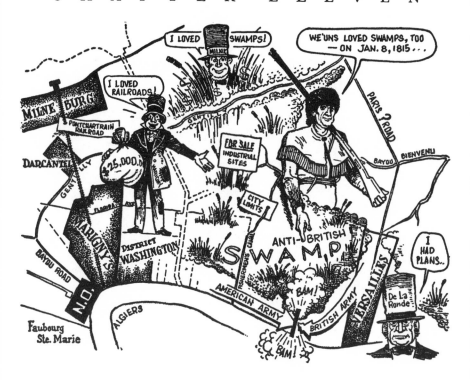

CHAPTER ELEVEN

Downtown Was
the Battleground

DOWNTOWN WAS

THE BATTLE-

GROUND

*L*ATE in the summer of 1814, a British fleet burned Washington, D. C., then came south for the winter to make things even hotter for New Orleans.

En route the fleet was joined by a convoy jam-packed with veteran troops who had just beaten Napoleon at Waterloo, and the Duke of Wellington's brother-in-law commanded them. On December 14, when this squadron stood off the shores of Lake Borgne, British naval units on the horizon were as many as the fishing boats which now dot the waters of that lake any sunny summer week-end. But the next thirty days were to prove no fishing trip for General Edward Pakenham, the brother-in-law, and his landing party of British regulars.

To begin with, Pakenham overestimated the force of General Andrew Jackson who was waiting for him in downtown New Orleans, and he underestimated the downtown's swamps. His force got so bogged down as it wallowed through the swamp from the lakeshore to the riverbank below the city, that historians have never been able to agree on their number. The most painstaking authority places them at something under 10,000 wet but willing troopers.

Then Pakenham delayed his attack, and while the British army dried out, Jackson established his line at the Rodrigues canal. At this point downtown, cypress morasses began only 1600 feet back from the river. Here, with his flanks secured, Jackson had a short line of concentrated fire power that ranks among the strongest fortified positions in military annals; this General Pakenham learned the hard way in twenty minutes on the morning of January 8, 1815.

But these conditions which made the downtown so good for military defense restricted its use for human habitation. Unlike uptown, where the river curls back forming a semi-circle of high ground along its bank; there it twists away, leaving a narrower shelf of habitable land. Earliest settlement huddled close to the river, only one ribbon of development thrusting out backward toward Lake Pontchartrain. Besides, down there was Bernard Marigny, who had quarreled with the American promoters seeking to join with him in developing the downtown.

Paradoxically, New Orleans may now thank Marigny (and thank the swamps too) for reserving this section of the city for industrial use. Today, downtown New Orleans is the only section in which sizable industries might find location. There the Industrial Canal, dug in 1923; and the proposed seaway, which will lateral off this canal to the Gulf, further earmark the downtown for industrialization already underway.

The Pontchartrain Railroad made possible the single ribbon of development downtown, which ventured back from the riverside. This was the first railroad west of the Alleghenies, the first of all American railroads to complete its trackage (all 4.96 miles of its "system"), and definitely an answer to the prayers of Bernard Marigny.

Authorized January 10, 1830, built in sixteen months, the Pontchartrain was a successful railroading adventure from the start. These were boom times in New Orleans; money was plentiful. But, alas, at this same time Bernard Marigny's princely inheritance was beginning to crack under the strains of his elegant extravagance. He was mortgaged at the Citizens Bank for $280,000, and other debts put him into the red for $40,000 more. But now the railroad was to run out Elysian Fields all the way to the lake, almost half of its length through Marigny's land! Immediately, he received $25,000 for the right-of-way; and, immediately too, he began projecting his Faubourg New Marigny further back into the swamp, alongside the tracks. On the downtown side of Elysian Fields, Cousin d'Estrahan, who somehow had acquired this part of the Marigny estate, began the subdivision of Faubourg Franklin.

Thus, while it was Marigny's creditors who stimulated partition of his estate, and the railroad which made partition practical, it was unquestionably that fabulous old Creole, with his flare for the flamboyant, who named the new streets which resulted.

First, however, it is to be observed that the streets which ran back from the river in Faubourg Marigny were continued, in alignment and name, into the newer subdivisions. Now consider the crossing streets. Who but unpredictable Marigny would fasten upon a row of streets such irrelevant names as Treasure, Abundance, Agriculture, Industry, Duels, Hope, Law, Magistrate, Virtue, Force, Liberal, and Genius. These were a dozen cross streets in the new suburbs, and the first seven continue so called. (Magistrate, Virtue, Force, Liberal, and Genius became actual continuations of streets crossing Canal street, and have since been changed to Dorgenois, Rocheblave, Tonti, Miro, and Galvez). Nine other cross streets in these faubourgs, with one exception, have similarly been changed to continue names borne on the other side of St. Bernard avenue—the upperline of Faubourg New Marigny, and named for Bernard Marigny. Because Urquhart street does not continue beyond this avenue, it alone in this group of nine retains its original name, the name of Thomas Urquhart, prominent capitalist and director in the Citizens Bank.

Today, on the map, Florida Avenue is shown much wider below Elysian Fields. There it was the original Florida Walk of Faubourg Franklin. Above Elysian Fields, it was Marigny Avenue of New Marigny. Since 1923 the whole street is Florida with its designation changed from "walk" to "avenue"; unchanged, though, is its great breadth below Elysian Fields—438 feet between property lines, widest dedicated street in the city.

But, alas, Faubourg Franklin's two most fascinating contributions to the nomenclature are lost. In the extreme northeast corner of the suburb were two short streets named—Madmen and Amen! And yet, Madmen and Amen streets are not wholly lost. Far to the north, at the lakeside terminal of the Pontchartrain Railroad, their names are still officially retained in the street nomenclature of Milneburg.

There the railroad intruded upon the swampy privacy of Alexander Milne, who owned most of the lakeshore in 1830. This odd Scot declared the swampland to be exceedingly healthy, and proved it by living to be eighty. He amassed a fortune in swampy real estate operations and brick-making enterprises, and took a singularly active interest in his lakeside subdivision, seeking to make it homelike for strangers by naming the streets there for many a faraway city. And one of the parks he labeled Strangers' Square!

Milneburg's main street was Edinburgh, after the chief city of Milne's native land. In 1923 its name was ruthlessly changed to—of all things—Hibernia; there happened already to be an Edinburgh street in Carrollton. Other streets which Milne named for cities include: Hamburg, Paris, Brussels, Warsaw, now changed to Republic, Havana, New Orleans, Madrid, Vienna, New York, and Pressburg. Curiously, Brussels street is retained in the nomenclature with its French spelling, Bruxelles—and pronounced "Brux-cells," which is neither French nor English.

For Alexander Milne, Milneburg was profitable. Speculators bought his land; John Slidell reputedly paid $5,000 in gold for a few choice lots, which were still swampy a hundred years later when the drainage of the remote section became a WPA project. Not until the time of World War II was Milneburg more than a resort, huddled on the lake end of Elysian Fields. Then war housing was built there.

One other subdivision, resulting from the railroad, was Darcantel, midway between the river and lake at the intersection of Elysian Fields and Gentilly Road. All that remains of Darcantel, now completely enveloped by the city on all sides, are a few cross street names it contributed: Carnot, Stephen Girard, Pelopidas, Caton, and Foy. A real Creole jambalaya is this list: Carnot was a French general, Stephen Girard a French-American financier, Pelopidas a general of ancient Thebes, Caton a Roman book of ethics, and Foy a neighbor!

Along the river, below Enghein, Marigny's lower line, was the Faubourg Washington, actually a consolidation of six lesser faubourgs, called Districts. These were Daunois, Montegut, De Clouet, Montreuil, Cariby, and deLesseps; all named for men whose plantations they had been.

It was Nicholas Daunois, who named three streets for the forts Carondelet built around New Orleans, of which only St. Ferdinand remains so called. St. Charles and St. Louis were changed to Port and Cotton Press, or Press. Equally as old as Daunois' was the subdivision of Alexander De Clouet. Both were carved with streets at the time of the Battle of New Orleans. Colonel De Clouet, a descendant of Alexander, was the official courier between the territorial legislature and General Jackson. Jackson wanted to shoot him when he brought tidings that the legislature was voting to surrender the city to avoid property damage. Besides a street named Clouet, Louisa and Piety remain of the original names. Louisa was named for a De Clouet; and Piety, which is a corruption of the name Piété, may also have belonged to that ancient colonial family.

But the downtown streets, of which there are forty from Enghein (or Almonaster, as it is now called) to the lower city limits make their chief contributions to the historical nomenclature for the relations many bear to the battle at

Chalmette. After all, the downtown was the battleground. Jackson's second line of defense, prepared for him to fall back on should his line at the Rodrigues canal be broken, was in the District Montreuil, where Congress and Independence streets now appear. His headquarters were in the house of Bartholomew Macarty, on the adjoining plantation. Robert Gautier Montreuil later named two other streets cut through his land for two of his daughters, Désirée and Elmire; and the subdivision of Macarty's land honored two other Creole belles, Pauline Forstall and Jeanne Macarty. But, because the names were used elsewhere for streets, in 1894 Jeanne was changed to Alvar, and Elmire became Gallier in 1923. The Galliers, father and son, were famous New Orleans architects of the Greek Revival period; Alvar is just a name.

Through a muddled translation into English, Désirée street has become Desire; and the famous "Streetcar Named Desire," which crossed both Frenchmen and the street once called Good Children en route between Canal and Desire streets, has become a bus! Désirée Montreuil moved away from all this when she married Francois de La Barre, for whom Labarre Road in Metaire is named.

The origin of Poland, an important downtown cross street, is obscure. The street was cut through a tract of land owned by George Selkeld, British consul in New Orleans during the 1830's. But Sister street, on the other side of the Industrial Canal, marks this neighborhood as one of the three locations of the convent of the Ursulines, since that order came to New Orleans in 1727. On Ursulines street, in the Vieux Carré, the nuns were domiciled for ninety years, here they remained until 1912 when the present convent was built uptown on State street.

While still in the Vieux Carré, the convent served as a hospital at the time of the battle. On January 8, 1815, when the fighting raged below the city, the Abbé Dubourg was celebrating a solemn mass of supplication and aid in the convent chapel. A statue of Our Lady of Prompt Succor was displayed on the altar. News of victory arrived before the mass was over; and in commemoration of this God-given victory, Sister Ste. Marie, Mother Superior of the convent, made her famous vow. Forever after, on each January 8, a mass of Thanksgiving to Our Lady would be celebrated in the convent chapel: and so it has been. A few years after this, a new street was dedicated in the American Section of the city, and named for Our Lady of Prompt Succor. It is still called, untranslated from the French, Notre Dame street.

As for other downtown streets, the names of several have been changed to other names meaningless to the story of the region. French became France, because it was too similar to Frenchmen; St. Maurice, Alabo, Lamanche, Tupelo, Japonica, and Kentucky have no stories to tell. But every other downtown street bears the names of men who lived there, or owned plantations there, and most of whom fought the Redcoats when the downtown was the battleground.

St. Claude, the main downtown artery which used to be Good Children street, crosses the city limits into the lower parish to become the St. Bernard Highway. After a few minutes' ride, the Rodrigues canal is reached, the actual battlefield crossed, and the highway forks to pass on both sides of the ruins of the plantation house of Peter De La Ronde. Here, on the other side of the battlefield, another story can be told—not a pro-British story, but one that is certainly pro-De La Ronde.

On his twenty-first birthday, young Peter planted the double row of majestic oaks, which led from his house to the riverbank. These have been called the Pakenham Oaks ever since somebody started the story that "mortally wounded Pakenham died under them." All historians deny this, but most everybody still calls them after the bullet-ridden brother-in-law of the Duke of Wellington. Peter De La Ronde was forty-three when he played a prominent part in the battle of New Orleans. Afterwards, probably pleased with his trees, De La Ronde set out to plant cities; one on the river to be called Versailles; another across the swamp on Lake Borgne to be called Paris. A barge canal and a road would connect these two metropolises, which De La Ronde loudly proclaimed would soon outstrip New Orleans. But, unlike his oak trees, De La Ronde's cities never took root. Besides the subdivision of his plantation into the village of Versailles, all that remains of the grandiose scheme is Paris Road, named for the city that never was.

Today, black-topped Paris Road, which connects St. Bernard Highway with Gentilly Highway, provides an interesting back door to the downtown, and the battleground, of New Orleans.

Back-of-Town
Was Backward

BACK-OF-TOWN

WAS BACKWARD

SEPTEMBER 14, 1874, marked the end of carpetbag rule in New Orleans. Not long after this a local writer was commissioned to do a piece about the city for a national magazine. To illustrate his article, this writer had a photograph taken of the exact geographical center of the city, thus to show realistically how desolate and forbidding were many sections of the back-of-town. His story went on to tell of excellent duck hunting, alligator stalking, and fishing all within the 150 square miles of the corporate limits. There were many instances, he wrote, of men becoming hopelessly lost, and perishing, in the trackless cypress swamps within New Orleans' boundaries.

The editors willingly accepted his story, but indignantly rejected the photograph. No place could be so weird and gloomy, was their sharp criticism, and be the center of a great city. They frankly warned him of dire consequences which befel¹ authors who perpetrated hoaxes upon publishing houses.

The section this writer had selected for the geographical

center of the municipality, and photographed, was between Bienville and Conti streets two blocks back of City Park Avenue! During World War II, the famous Higgins Boat Plant was located there.

Reason for the slow development of the back-of-town was the problem which plagued New Orleans for the first 177 years of its history—drainage of the region. Most sections of modern New Orleans are still below high water in the river and the lake. Rain water must be syphoned from the city streets. Nine pumping stations—the world's largest —lift and relift rainfall, until it will flow off into Lakes Borgne and Pontchartrain. As early as 1835, the municipal government was seeking ways to drain the back-of-town, which because of its close proximity would be extremely valuable if it were not so wet.

There was, however, one ribbon of development back there not retarded by the swampy terrain. Bayou Road— the ancient portage—was a well settled street long before the days of American domination. Trim plantation homes lined its way from the rear of the Vieux Carré to the Place Bretonne. At Place Bretonne, which is today dominated by the Lebreton Market, the lawless meandering of Bayou Road was brought to an abrupt halt by the three earliest back-of-town suburbs. Most important of these, and the largest, was Faubourg St. John—a subdivision of part of the huge estate of Daniel Clark. It was made by Barthelemy Lafon in 1809.

Here at Place Bretonne the old portage was redesigned to fork into four directions. To the left went Dorgenois street, through the property of Francois Joseph LeBreton D'Orgenois; straight ahead two streets through the Faubourg St. John continued the road to the bayou—these were St. John and Washington, changed now to Bell and De Soto. The fourth fork was Gentilly Road, which flanked both Daniel Clark's subdivision and that of Blanque and Fortin.

This last suburb, called Faubourg Pontchartrain, is interesting for the accurate manner in which its streets tell its history. Grand Route St. John, the main street, comes nearest to being Bayou Road's original continuation to the bayou. Because the suburb was named for the old Count of Pontchartrain, another street honors his son, the Count of Maurepas. There is less significance to the third running street, called Florida, now changed to Ponce de Leon. Faubourg Pontchartrain marks the spot where the Houmas Indians were found encamped when the first white men came; here, too, the French workmen encamped when they arrived to clear the site for Bienville's city. It was fitting that a crossing street should be named Encampment; historians shake their heads sadly when they learn the street has been changed to N. Lopez—which street it vaguely continues. It is further regrettable that another called Swamp street—so symbolic of all the back-of-town—has been changed to N. White. However Sauvage street remains; and also does Mystery street, whose origin—properly enough—is something of a mystery.

Between Daniel Clark's suburb and the tract of D'Orgenois, Surveyor Lafon allowed sufficient width for the street to include a drainage ditch. Here was set a pattern for subdivisions that followed for which modern New Orleans may well be grateful. Planned to meet the economic needs of that period—to drain the tracts—these broad streets are now admirably fitted to economic requirements of the present era. Today these streets, with their canals underground, are the wide automobile boulevards which crisscross the city. It is strikingly appropriate that this first broad street was called, and still is called, Broad street!

Daniel Clark was certainly the father of back-of-town development. It was also proven certain that he was the father of Myra Clark. But the years-long efforts of his daughter to prove this latter paternity ranks second only to the swamps in stalling the growth of the back-of-town. A confusing man was Daniel Clark.

This young Irishman was brought to New Orleans in 1786 by his uncle, for whom Clarksdale, Mississippi, is named. In the last dozen years of Spanish rule, young Daniel made a fortune as a merchant and importer. He became an American citizen in order to become American consul at New Orleans, and he is generally credited to have been first to suggest to President Jefferson that he buy Louisiana. Clark was always buying things himself, usually getting as good a bargain as did Jefferson when he bought Louisiana. As his operations extended he took in two of his clerks, Richard Relf and Beverly Chew, as partners; and these three made outstanding contributions to New Orleans commerce, contributions in which Messrs. Clark, Relf and Chew unfailingly shared in a material way. They were sharp operators, these three.

Clark died suddenly in 1813, and his two partners commenced operations on his estate in the customary ways of the firm. Nobody knows exactly what happened in Clark's house in the hour following his death, and nobody knows what happened to Clark's last will and testament in that hour. It was proven to the satisfaction of no less prudent an authority than the United States Supreme Court that there was a last will; but two days after the funeral, sorrowing partner Relf—he had been chief mourner at the bedside—filed for probate what was later judged to be, again in the opinion of the United States Supreme Court, a second-to-last will and testament. After ordering all just debts paid, this will instructed that the residue of the estate go to Clark's mother. Relf and Chew were the executors. The estate was liquidated with what was later judged unseeming haste; and also the amount of just debts owed to partners Relf and Chew were considerable.

Clark was never married, it was believed. Always he explained that he was so busy, such late office hours, so many long business trips. But like many another tired businessman, Daniel Clark had his moments of relaxation. One of these was Zulime. Zulime Carriere appears to have made up in physical attraction what she so sadly lacked in good judgment. Even in court proceedings the numerous testimonies that can be summed up to say Zulime was "beautiful—and how," are recorded without objection from the alert opposition. And next to twenty percent interest, nothing affected Daniel Clark so strongly as a beautiful woman. Only, Zulime was married to Jerry Des Grange.

This detail does not appear to have disturbed Daniel; and as for Zulime, her limited knowledge of English seemingly did not include the word "no." Daniel and Zulime were the very, very, very best of friends.

Then it became known that Husband Jerry already had a wife in Philadelphia. Full of curiosity, Zulime journeyed to the City of Brotherly Love for proof of this. Although the priest had died, and the church had burned down, Zulime somehow became convinced that Jerry was the husband of one Barbara Jeanbelle de Orcy. Daniel suddenly arrived in Philadelphia on a business trip, and he and Zulime were married.

This was a secret marriage. It was so secret that even Zulime and Daniel appeared entirely unconscious of it a few years later. She married one of the witnesses to Jerry's wedding and moved to France; also, when Daniel died, he was engaged to be married to another girl.

But up to this time Zulime had definitely become the mother of three children, although it was not at first definite whose were Jerry's and whose were Daniel's. This last the United States Supreme Court finally settled, but it took sixty-five years of litigation and cost—well, it cost $30,000 alone to print the 8,000 pages of closely written court records. The remarkable woman who instigated this litigation, longest and most turbulent in the history of American courts, was Myra Clark, youngest of these three children.

It was revealed that in 1803 Clark brought Zulime out to a cottage in his Faubourg St. John. She was expecting a baby, and Clark made careful arrangements. He engaged the services of a business associate, Samuel Davis, to shroud the birth with a maximum of secrecy. Davis' association with Clark was that of manager. He often operated an enterprise in his own name which Clark owned with Clark's identity in the matter never revealed. Such a project was the Davis Rope Walk on Canal street, between Decatur and Bourbon. And certainly another was the birth of Myra. She was born on the neighboring plantation of Mrs. Davis' brother, and nursed at the breast of Mrs. Davis. Later she went to live in Philadelphia with the Davises and was known as Myra Davis until she was twenty-five. Then she accidentally discovered the unusual circumstances of her birth.

Soon after this, numerous property owners in New Orleans discovered unusual circumstances in the titles to their real estate. For Myra appeared in town and claimed all the property Daniel Clark had owned when he died seventeen years earlier. It amounted to about one third of New Orleans! Richard Relf disputed that she was Clark's daughter; and, if she was, she could not be his legitimate daughter. Consequently, she had no legal right to claim or inherit anything. So Myra Clark went to court.

And when Myra Clark went to court it was unlike anybody else in the history of jurisdiction or jurisprudence. She stayed in court! She wore out two husbands, two entire U. S. Supreme Courts, and two whole generations of judges and lawyers in the lower courts. In the end she won. Her heritage was immense, but so were her expenses. In a material way, Myra Clark Gaines—as she was called through most of her litigation—made only a fair living out of her years in court—and so did numerous members of the legal profession. Mostly, Myra battled and won that richest of all treasures, a good name.

Myra would be a good name for a street in New Orleans. But there isn't any.

Of all Daniel Clark's property, Faubourg St. John was the section from which his daughter received most of her inheritance. Today it is a confusing neighborhood, its streets in such juxtaposition with all others, it seems as though the long legal warring had knocked them cock-eyed. Also, Ursulines street and Esplanade Avenue have been slashed right through Lafon's orderly plan of 1809, thus adding to the confusion.

It is interesting, however, that the street named for

Daniel Clark's best friend and executor of his purloined will, Colonel Bellechasse, has been retained in the nomenclature. Retained, also, is Lepage street which recalls Le-Page DuPratz, colonial settler in the neighborhood; and winding Crete street near-by is not named for the Mediterranean island, but for a *crête*, or crest, which once distinguished the terrain there. Orchid street was formerly Oak; and St. John street which was changed to Bell, honors H. H. Bell, City Surveyor in 1873. Except for Port street, on the bayou, the crossing streets were numbered: First, Second, etc. None has been retained. And Port was changed to Moss in 1895.

So, besides the swamp, litigation delayed development of the back-of-town. Myra Clark Gaines' was not the only legal free-for-all fought in its squashy environs, nor was it the first. In the middle 1830's New Orleans was experiencing a wild, inflationary period. Real estate changed hands with the rapidity of a fast infield effecting a double play. These were the years, prior to the Panic of 1837, that developed the uptown section; and during these years large areas of the back-of-town began to appear on maps with city streets—even though surveyors had to splash waist deep to line them up.

Notable among these subdivisions was John Arrowsmith's Faubourg Jackson. Arrowsmith acquired from Ferdinand d'Hebecourt all the land now fronting on City Park Avenue from Bayou St. John to St. Patrick's Cemetery. At first he divided the tract into forty-six slices, each ninety feet wide, all fronting on City Park Avenue. This street was then called Metairie Road; it actually was the continuation of the road alongside Bayou Metairie.

After disposing of some slices nearest Bayou St. John, Arrowsmith engaged Zimpel to subdivide the remainder in order to make his faubourg dovetail with the street alignments of Carrollton, from which Arrowsmith was separated by only one tract. The slices which Arrowsmith first disposed of are today another small neighborhood where the streets run counter to the general pattern. Streets such as Taft, Wilson, Bungalow, Sherwood Forest, etc., are easy to get lost in.

After Zimpel divided the remainder, an interesting lawsuit resulted. Arrowsmith sought to claim the value of *ALL* his streets which ran into the swamps beyond his lines. How the lawsuit resulted is not important here; suffice to say that the streets do continue.

And here once again Surveyor Zimpel has left his signature,—a running over enthusiasm for Napoleon which has spilled into the streets of every major subdivision of Zimpel's design. In Bouligny, he left Napoleon Avenue and other streets named for Napoleonic victories; in Carrollton several field marshals were mustered into the nomenclature—Ney, Cambronne, Murat, and Bernadotte. But Arrowsmith's Faubourg Jackson was reserved for only the tip-top echelon of *Le Grand Armee*—only the crowned heads! Here a street was named for Emperor Napoleon and two others for King Bernadotte of Sweden and King Murat of Italy, marshals whom Napoleon had so promoted. Fittingly associated with the best of Bonaparte, in Zimpel's opinion, were David and Solomon—great kings of Judea; and Alexander The Great. All are street names, and with them in the suburb are less original contributions to the nomenclature as St. Patrick, St. Anthony, and Olympia; while tucked farthest back in the plan is a street named St. Helene, isle of Napoleon's banishment. He was also banished from Faubourg Jackson in 1894, when Napoleon street was changed to Hennessy, New Orleans chief of police who had been assassinated by the Mafia four years earlier. The city decided one Napoleon Avenue (in Bouligny) was enough.

Certainly, the most interesting personality speculating in back-of-town real estate during the 1830's was Marie Joseph Paul Yvers Roch Gilbert Du Motier, Marquis de La Fayette. He was back there because of the French revolution. General Lafayette wanted and would accept nothing for his time and money expended in winning the American War of Independence. Lafayette had plenty—until the French people beheaded Louis XVI, and sought to do likewise with every aristocrat they could catch. It was different with Lafayette who had fought for Liberty; he escaped with his head but not his fortune.

In 1794, the U. S. Congress voted him $24,424, his back pay as major general in the Continental Army. Lafayette was grateful and also uneconomical; soon he was broke again. In Congress committees were appointed to figure out ways to help this man who had helped America. It had to be done with dignity; Lafayette would never accept charity. This was agreeable with Congress in 1800, as the United States was in no financial position to be charitable.

It so happened at this time there was a bill in Congress to do something for the boys who had won the war—the Revolutionary War. The scheme was to give them land, acres of it. As a general, Lafayette was entitled to 11,500. The land to be thus awarded was located north of the Ohio river. Good land to homestead on, and in the long run it could be sold for quite a profit. But Lafayette needed something he could quickly turn into dollars and pounds and francs. Homestead! Lafayette was no Daniel Boone!

So the law was amended to apply also to Louisiana, newly purchased from France. There were rumors that Lafayette might even move to America; Jefferson offered him the post of Governor of Louisiana. In reply Lafayette was courteous and noncommittal. He accepted the land in Louisiana, and appointed Armand Duplantier to select for him at least one part of his grant near to New Orleans. Once Calliope street from Coliseum to the river was named Duplantier, because for a while this man was owner of the Faubourg Delord. Duplantier's task for Lafayette was not easy. Most of the land near New Orleans had been distributed by French and Spanish grants, which the United States was obliged to respect.

Finally, on April 7, 1806, Duplantier filed a warrant for a thousand acres described as follows: "On the lands belonging to the United States and lying around the City of New Orleans including the fortifications in the parts thereof not received by the government and on the Canal Carondelet as far as the Macarty plantation."

This amounted to giving to Lafayette all the land on both sides of present-day Canal street as far over as Common street on one side and Iberville on the other; all the lake side of North Rampart street between Tulane and Lafitte (the Carondelet Canal), as far back as about North Galvez.

There was a mighty squawk!

The Corporation of the City of New Orleans screamed that it owned 1,800 feet beyond the fortifications according to some old law of Governor Carondelet. Also, it was pointed out the land Duplantier had filed did not add up to 1,000 acres; and the law stipulated that no less than 1,000-acre tracts could be granted.

Back to Congress went President Jefferson, and the law was tailored to suit Lafayette's needs—and also accommodate available real estate in New Orleans. Congress also appeased the Corporation of the City of New Orleans, by an act in 1807 wherein it recognized the city's ownership of the commons adjacent to it—providing the city would relinquish all its other claims about the old law and Governor Carondelet and the 1,800 feet. This was the Act of Congress which provided for the street with the Canal on it. See the chapter, "Canal Street and Contrasts."

Once again Duplantier filed for Lafayette on vacant land back-of-town, back of the fortifications. He filed for 520 acres. The remainder of Lafayette's grant was secured in cotton lands around Pointe Coupee. It was Lafayette's plan to sell his New Orleans land quickly for money he so badly needed, and hold on to his cotton plantation for his children. But things happened differently; he was able to sell the plantation for $12 an acre. This left him free of debt, and free to speculate with his New Orleans grant. He entered into partnership with a Sir John Coghill, and unloaded two thirds of the 520 acres on this British knight for $15,895. Then, to Lafayette's consternation, it was discovered that there were not 520 acres in the tract of which Sir John had bought two thirds! At this point Sir John died.

Sir Josiah Coghill, a nephew, inherited the two thirds of something less than 520 acres. A new warrant correcting the tract to the 503 $88/100$ acres it contained was delivered to Lafayette, all signed and sealed with the great seal of the

United States. But more consternation awaited Lafayette. Other owners of the "back-of-town" began checking their lines; then it was revealed that perfectly valid prior claims in the vicinity of this tract shrunk the $5038\frac{8}{100}$ acres of supposedly vacant land to actually only $1147\frac{4}{100}$ acres!

Embarrassed Lafayette offered to give it all to Sir Josiah, or give him 500 acres of Florida real estate he owned. But Sir Josiah stoutly stuck to the partnership, with his two thirds interest in a 520-acre tract which now measured less than 115 acres. He kept his eyes open, though, and unloaded his interests on John Hagan of New Orleans for $26,640.

So John Hagan became Lafayette's partner. He immediately offered to subdivide Lafayette's one-third along with his two thirds. He would do this for only two thirds of the profits of Lafayette's one third interest. Lafayette agreed. This left him with a one third interest in one third of his subtracted tract. Then he died.

Hagan bought the interests of Lafayette's two daughters, but a son refused to sell his share. The resulting subdivision, call Faubourg Hagan, was sold out to home seekers during 1840-41. Lafayette's son then received his share of the profits derived from 13 acres, which was his one third inheritance of his father's one third interest in one third of his investment in back-of-town New Orleans. Lafayette was a much better major general than a real estate speculator.

Faubourg Hagan consisted of 41 city blocks, in whole or part, in a triangular area between Claiborne and Galvez on Tulane, and coming to a point near Orleans and Claiborne. It is to be observed, too, that half of this Lafayette tract, and the final development of it—Faubourg Hagan—

lay within land Myra Clark later declared was her inheritance!

Because the back-of-town developed late, the names which have settled upon the streets which cross Canal present a pot-pourri of New Orleans history.

Beyond Rampart (the old city's rampart) is Basin street. Across Canal this street is called Saratoga, except for the first block which is Elk Place. The Elks Club was here, and though the B.P.O.E. lost possession of their building, and moved, the street continues to be Elk.

Crozat is the next street on the downtown side. It was changed to this name of the first lessee of French Louisiana from Franklin, its original name. On the uptown side, this street is Loyola.

Liberty is next, first called Treme, for Claude Treme, owner of all the land on the downtown side of Lafitte street. The two streets following Liberty are Villere and Robertson, which recall Jacques Philippe Villere and William B. Robertson, second and third governors of Louisiana. Wide Claiborne street, which is next, pays its respects to the only governor of the Territory of Louisiana and first chief executive of the State.

Fourth Louisiana governor was Henry Johnson, who was followed by Pierre Derbigny. Then came Andre Bienvenu Roman and Edward D. White. Except for White, which is further out, these are next crossing streets. Governor White was the father of United States Chief Justice White.

Two Spanish governors came next, and beyond Galvez and Miro is a street named for Henri Tonti. An Italian soldier of fortune, Tonti stood side by side with LaSalle when he proclaimed Louisiana a French possession. When LaSalle got lost in the wilderness, Tonti spent years searching for him and finally found Iberville and Bienville. He served with them until his death in 1704. Of Tonti Governor Claiborne had this to say: "No character in the romantic history of French exploration in North America is so uniformly perfect and admirable."

But the romantic history of the man for whom the next street appears to have been named was confined to the wife of M. Rochemore, civil affairs administrator in the time of Governor Kerlerec. It was this Rochemore and his wife who headed the cabal to wreck Kerlerec's government. Madame Rochemore it was who wrote malicious, risqué songs in ridicule of the Governor, songs which so infuriated Kerlerec. Rocheblave, of the Swiss Guard, was Madame Rochemore's lover; it is not clear why a street is named for him.

The street named for LeBreton D'Orgenois is next. He is fully entitled to representation in the nomenclature; not only was this his land, but he was the first U. S. Marshal of the territorial government; also he was president pro tem of the Territorial Legislature in 1812, and acting mayor of New Orleans for one month.

Next is Broad street, which separated the lands of D'Orgenois and Daniel Clark—the first broad street. Dupré street, which follows behind White honors another acting governor in 1830—Jacques Dupré.

Then follow two Spanish governors and two Royal Intendants. In Spanish colonial government, the intendant was second in charge. He wasn't the governor's lieutenant; rather his job was to keep an eye on the governor and administer civil affairs. The two governors represented here are Gayoso and Salcedo; the two intendants, Rendon and Lopez.

The next street is the city's second widest. (Florida Avenue below Almonaster, is the widest.) Originally called Hagan Avenue, it is now Jefferson Davis; and the next street is now named for Daniel Clark. Formerly it was called Whiskey street . . . Clark and whiskey! Both have caused headaches to Orleanians.

Lemon used to be the name of the next street, now called Genois in recollection of Joseph Genois, Recorder for the Second Municipality in the 1840's. And Mulberry used to be the name of the following cross street, now called Telemachus, for the Greek who spent his young manhood looking for his father, Ulysses, who couldn't find his way home from the Trojan War.

Completing the cross streets to Carrollton Avenue are Cortez, named for the Spaniard; and Scott and Pierce, for U. S. presidents. Then beyond Carrollton, and the next nine streets which John Arrowsmith sponsored, is City Park Avenue, which used to be Metairie Road. This is the end of Canal street.

When it continues to the lake as Canal Boulevard, only the post office seems aware that the first block of that boulevard isn't Canal at all. It is Wedell Place—for the Louisiana aviation pioneer who lost his life.

And properly, City Park Avenue ends the region popularly called back-of-town in New Orleans. Beyond is Lakeview, a comparatively new section. When back-of-town was swamps, Lakeview was unexplored territory. Eccentric Alexander Milne once owned most of it; and there is a Milne street in Lakeview.

CHAPTER THIRTEEN

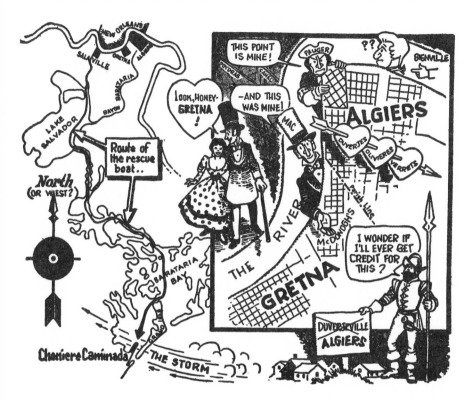

Across
the Main Street

ACROSS

THE MAIN STREET

Snug behind its west bank levee, Algiers is part of New Orleans and yet apart from it. It is as though some mischievous Genie impishly tacked certain similar characteristics on all New Orleans neighborhoods, then missed the ferry when it came Algiers' turn. There is still no other way in the city to reach Algiers than via ferry; and that westbank community retains a remoteness and a difference all its own.

Today Algiers is the fifteenth ward of the city, comprising the Fifth Municipal District, with an historical record every bit as ancient as New Orleans. But its record has been poorly kept, and only fragmentary is actual knowledge of Algiers' early days.

To begin with, it is not definitely known how it got its name. Officially called Duverjeville (also Duverjeburg) for the first three decades of American domination in Louisiana, one of the earliest appearances in print of its name as Algiers is the New Orleans City Directory of 1840. Thirty years later, on March 14, 1870, when the community was formally incorporated into the city of New Orleans, it knew no other name.

But the association of this neighborhood with its unusual name dates back, with legendary insistence, to the beginning of Spanish rule. William H. Seymour's paperbound booklet, "The Story of Algiers," enjoys the distinction of being the best history of the village. It is the only one. Seymour relates how an old citizen named Lululla often said Algiers' name was suggested by one of O'Reilly's soldiers, who had come to Louisiana fresh from service against the pirates of Algeria. In itself, this would not be sufficient reason for the acquisition of the name. But other circumstances contributed.

In the beginning, Bienville sought and was granted all of the Chapitoulas from the Commons to Nine Mile Point, or all of present-day Uptown and Carrollton, plus another tract on the opposite bank of the river. Roughly, the boundaries of Bienville's westbank concession was all of Algiers of today, bounded on the upper side by Powder street, and extending back on the line of that street as far as Farnum Road.

Some historians slyly point out that Bienville was so insistent upon establishing New Orleans where he did to enhance the value of his lands.

In 1721, two years after Bienville's grants were approved, Adrian de Pauger sliced off for himself a pie-shaped piece of the governor's westbank concession. This eighteenth century claim jumping, by the engineer who had laid out the original city of New Orleans, is perpetually retained on the map of the city. The twenty-two squares of

Algiers, bounded by Opelousas and Verret streets, which are in juxtaposition with all other squares, comprise the bulk of Pauger's slice.

What the Royal Engineer had engineered for himself was not discovered until three years later, when the Company of the West sought to buy this very section, directly across the river from the city. Bienville is reported to have been exceedingly distressed to find Pauger squatting on his land. He pointed out that there was much other vacant land for Pauger to file on, without filing on top of him, Bienville. But Pauger objected to being removed. In turn, he pointed out (1) that he had spent money "improving" the point; and (2) Bienville already had plenty of land.

However, the city council decided Bienville was the lawful owner, and ordered that Pauger move, and that the governor pay him for the alleged "improvements."

Adrian de Pauger died before the matter was finally settled. Historians take pains to point out that this land argument did not alienate Bienville and Pauger's affection for each other; and in his will Pauger left Bienville his guns and pistols. The historians do not explain whether they were loaded.

In 1728 many of the concessions granted by John Law's defunct Company of the West were cancelled by the king, then regranted in smaller plots, but only to those in actual possession of the lands and who had improved them. As Bienville was then in France, having been recalled by Delachaise's recommendation, he lost much of his property at this time.

The point across the river from the city, which Pauger had grabbed, had been appropriated by the company and later by the king for official use. The council of the colony voted a recommendation that Bienville be paid for this land, if, and when, the colony ever got any money. To all appearances it seems that Bienville was euchred out of his real estate, which later became the fifth ward of the city of New Orleans and called Algiers.

Along with much of the west bank as far up as Donaldsonville, the section was known for years as the King's Plantation, and Lepage Du Pratz was the manager. The point opposite New Orleans came to be called Point Antoine, and later Point Marigny. It was directly across the river from the great plantation home which Antoine Marigny built at the foot of present-day Elysian Fields Avenue. It was also popularly called Slaughter House Point, because the colonial abattoir was there.

Toward the end of French rule in the colony, the point was used principally as a depot for slaves, newly arrived from Africa. Here also the French established the powder magazine of the colony, which location the Spaniards retained when they came. Powder street, consequently, got its name from this. And the presence of many Negroes near that powder magazine, where the Spanish soldier was on guard duty, adds credence to the legend that first gave the region its sobriquet—Algiers.

At this time the original Algiers was in the heyday of its 300-year reign of piratical terror in the Mediterranean. One of the half-hearted punitive expeditions sent against the Algerian brigands by European powers was a mission assigned to the command of General Don Alexander O'Reilly—the same O'Reilly who came to take over Louisiana for Spain in 1769. So it is entirely possible for Old Citizen Lululla's story to be correct.

The Spaniards in Louisiana quickly disposed of all idle

Crown property, and the land across the river from New Orleans was granted to Louis Bonrepos, on condition that he improve it. This grant was made February 3, 1770. Bonrepos later sold it to Martial LeBoeuf, and on August 9, 1805 Barthelemy Duverje purchased the point from LeBoeuf for $18,000. A few days later, Duverje sold a section (nearest McDonoughville) to Toussaint Mossy. He also sold a plot exactly on the point to Andre Sequin for a shipyard. This is reputed to have been the first shipyard established on the coast of the Gulf of Mexico.

At this point, then, the colonial proprietors of Algiers Point were Bienville and Pauger, the Company of the West, The King of France (with Lepage Du Pratz as superintendent); briefly the Spanish Crown, then Louis Bonrepos, Martial LeBoeuf, Barthelemy Duverje, and Toussaint Mossy. Of all of these early owners, only one—LeBoeuf—has a street named for him in Algiers today.

It was during the ownership of the Duverjes that the region (which must have been popularly called Algiers even then) was subdivided into lots by Alan d'Hemicourt, and one of the streets which led to the shipyard named Sequin. Meanwhile, two other families had acquired adjoining plantations—the Oliviers and the Verrets. For several years Duverjes and Oliviers and Verrets were falling in love with each other, and after resulting weddings all were one big happy family. It is from members of this family circle that come most of the street names in the older section of Algiers, bounded by Opelousas Avenue and Valette street.

Alix Duverje married Jean Baptiste Olivier, hence Alix street and Olivier street. Evelina Duverje married Charles Godefroy Olivier, and there is an Evelina street. Elmira and Verret streets result from the romance of Elmira Olivier and Furcy Verret; and Eliza street recalls Elmira's sister who married Peter Delaverne. Even in-laws were honored, hence Delaverne street; and the original name of Pelican street was Peter. But alas, Barthelemy street has been changed to Bermuda; it had been named for Barthelemy Duverje, the daddy of all the Duverjes.

Perle Olivier was happily wedded to Jules Villere, and on the original plan the street named Morgan was Villere street. Just how Pierre Godefroy Bouny got his name on a street in this neighborhood, without marrying a Duverje or an Olivier or a Verret, is obscure. The fact that his middle name is the same as the middle name of Evelina's husband may have helped.

Originally, the street called Patterson was the Public Road. Captain Patterson was the naval hero of the Battle of New Orleans; and regardless of the Duverje-Olivier-Verret axis, Powder street continues so called because the colonial powder magazine was there.

Because of its location, Algiers was not long in becoming an important hub of transportation. Many of the present street names reflect a bustling, busy past which was Algiers'. Sequin with his shipyard belongs in this category, and so does Valette. Francois Valette was one of the members of the company that built the huge Brooklyn warehouses; he also operated Sequin's shipyard for a time, and in his honor a street named Gosselin was changed to Valette.

From the Belleville Ironworks comes Belleville street, as does Brooklyn from Valette's warehouses. Pelican street was named for a drydock, and Market street became Opelousas in the 1850's when the New Orleans, Opelousas and

Great Western Railroad was built to run from Algiers to "some point on the Sabine river." However, it never got any farther than Brashear City. After the Civil War, Charles Morgan acquired the railroad; and at this time Villere street was changed to Morgan, as was Brashear City, in St. Mary's Parish, changed to Morgan City. Whitney street in Algiers, incidentally, recalls Morgan's son-in-law; and one of his railroad's superintendents.

In time this railroad became part of the Southern Pacific System; and by 1900 the immense yards and wharves of the SP gave eloquent testimony to the fact that here, through Algiers, passed between seventy and seventy-five percent of all freight to and from the east and west coast of the United States! At these yards and docks transfers from freight train to steamship was made; often a whole train's cargo from the West was loaded aboard ship in twelve hours for the remainder of its journey to an Atlantic seaboard point. In recollection of this transcontinental traffic are Atlantic and Pacific streets, side by side in Algiers today. The opening of the Panama Canal brought an end to this ship-and-rail system of transcontinental freight, so much of which passed through Algiers.

Along with LeBoeuf are Thayer, Wagner, Hendee, and Sumner, who are all early landowners or prominent citizens of Algiers. Streets are named for them, as is also one for Martin Behrman, habitual (over 17 years) mayor of the city of New Orleans. Algiers was grateful to General Adolf Meyer, whose labors in Congress resulted in the Algiers Navy Yard. General Meyer Avenue flanks the Navy's property.

The remainder of Algiers street names follow no pattern and stop at nothing. The poet Homer, the mathematician

Newton, and the goddess Diana are three streets in a row. And perhaps Socrates would call for a second jigger of hemlock if he knew what has happened to the pronunciation of his name in the nomenclature of Algiers' streets! There are still a number of Negroes living in Algiers, and for much of its length Socrates street runs through Negro neighborhoods. Through constant usage, the name of the Greek philosopher has almost become a matter of public record with its new—and decidedly unGrecian—pronunciation of "so-KRATS."

A few blocks above Socrates street is the parish line, the limit of Algiers and New Orleans westbank corporate limits. Here begins Jefferson Parish, which was carved from Orleans Parish in 1807, and whose first suggested name was Tchoupitoulas Parish. But even though the westbank from the Algiers line to the Huey P. Long Bridge is out of bounds, its affairs and history are so tied in with New Orleans that this region must not go unmentioned. Besides its two incorporated communities have fascinating tales to tell . . .

As was the case with Algiers, Gretna and Westwego acquired the names they bear from their own enterprising activity, and discarded names first bestowed upon them. Gretna, which has been the seat of government for Jefferson Parish since 1884, had its beginning in 1827, when Nicholas Noel Destrehan settled some German immigrants on this land he owned. The village called Mechanicsham, consisted of a commons facing the river with two streets on each side. Destrehan permitted his settlers to set up their own local government, and all went well until one day one of the villagers borrowed Destrehan's pirogue without permission. Destrehan had the man soundly flogged by his slave-whipper. Thereupon the government of Mechanicsham slapped a $10,000 fine on its patron. It is said that the outraged scream of Nicholas Noel Destrehan could be heard across the river. He turned the town over to Jefferson Parish authorities and walked out. In their excitement, historians fail to mention whether he ever paid the $10,000 fine.

But the little community was not to be left to die on the vine, cut off from its fairy godfather. In 1838, the St. Mary's Market and Ferry Company received authorization to develop a larger townsite. It was to the ferry company's benefit to promote a prosperous community on the westbank— its ferries could then reap a revenue. That it succeeded is attested by a lengthy article in the *Daily Delta* of November 14, 1845, listing a foundry, a steam mill, carriage manufacturer, brickyard, a leading hotel, a public school, and other essentials of a bustling community. A ferry company did very well in the footsteps of a fairy godfather.

The name of Gretna appears to have first been fastened on the newer development adjoining Mechanicsham. And all indications are that the name crossed over from the New Orleans side, as did all the new growth. The quest for the origin of Gretna's name begins on the night of February 9, 1829 at the American Theater on Camp street. James H. Caldwell presented the farce by Beazley, "Gretna Green, Or A Trip to Scotland." This popular comedy was repeated in New Orleans theaters each season for the next twelve years; it was selected for the opening performance of the Carrollton House in 1841. Carrollton was then the seat of government of Jefferson Parish. The play was laid in Gretna Green, in Scotland, a village across the English border, and a famous haven for clandestine marriages from 1754 to 1856. Here it sufficed only for the couple to declare intention to wed in the presence of witnesses. It seems that the blacksmith's shop was the popular place for the declarations to be voiced. In 1826, more than two hundred such marriages were performed. Beazley was one of several playwrights of the time who employed the Gretna Green setting as the plot for a play.

Just what initial incident caused Gretna to be applied to the westbank community is not known. But in 1845 we read in the *Daily Delta;* ". . . Many inquiries have been made having for their object to learn whether the Gretna of Louisiana is anything like the Gretna of Scotland . . . there is no such blacksmith in our Gretna, but there is a worthy judge residing there who is at all times ready to perform so agreeable an office (as marriage) under the guarantees of the law."

D. McAfee, a Scotchman, was the Justice of the Peace in 1845. He was appointed to the office, and he also was in charge of the public school. Y. J. Lecorne was the first elected justice in 1866. Even though Gretna's convenient accommodations for run-away lovers does appear to have influenced its naming; marriages were not many until the time of Judge Michael Dauenhauer. In 1908 he distributed cards in New Orleans advertising his services. But by all counts, most marriages were performed by Judge George Trouth, who succeeded him. In 28 years this Justice of the Peace in Gretna legally hitched 18,985 loving couples!

Westwego, the other incorporated village on the westbank facing New Orleans, advertises itself to be the only American town whose name forms a complete sentence. As was the case of Algiers and Gretna, its name also began elsewhere and found it out. But not so far away as Algeria or Scotland is Chenière Caminada. Along the tattered southern coastline of Louisiana, a *chenière* is a curious geological indication of an even more complex subterranean underworld. Rising several feet above monotonous flat swamplands, these sandy bulwarks against the sea get their name from scrubby oak groves—chenières—which grow atop the reefs. In the days of Spanish domination, Grand Isle was profitably cultivated by Spanish sugarplanters, one of whom was Francisco Caminada. He built his home on the oak ridge across the pass from the island, and for him both the pass and the grove received their name, Caminada. After the Civil War, fisherfolk of Portugal, and the Philippines joined the French and Spanish already there; the generous sea provided living for them all. One village of these harvesters of the tide was Chenière Caminada, a prospering community of 1,500 inhabitants.

The sun never shone in the slaty skies on the morning of October 1, 1893. Shrieking winds pushed with increasing strength against the shacks and wharves. Fishing luggers pitched frantically at their moorings. And the sea itself—leady and opaque, as though to conceal its evil intentions—roared higher and higher up the beaches.

In the mounting fury, more than half of the lives in Chenière Caminada were forfeited. Eight hundred and twenty-two perished in that awful storm. Survivors had no thought other than to escape the twisted death and desolation which the hurricane left behind. To the west they would go, for that was the direction of higher ground from Chenière Caminada. It was in the tidal wave that most had perished.

The first boat to reach the agonized village came from Salaville, threading through the Company Canal, and down the labyrinth of waterways into Barataria Bay to Caminada. "West we go from here," distraught refugees cried again and again, "West we go!" They huddled aboard the boats, wet and broken and dazed from their fearful ordeal. The boats returned the way they had come, up Barataria, through Lakes Salvador and Cataouatche, and into the Company Canal to Salaville—the quickest way to food and shelter and medical attention.

Yet strangely the determination to go west from Chenière Caminada persisted in distracted minds. Somehow, as is the desperate resolution of people in great physical and mental torment and with fierce desire for survival, grim determination prevailed over every other thing, even the points of the compass.

Salaville was not west, but almost due north from illfated Chenière Caminada. Yet upon this haven, where they found comfort and warmth and sympathetic attention, feverish minds first fastened the name; Westwego.

And so it has remained; Westwego.

What are words? What are names? What use are they if they do not mean what those who say them intend them to mean? To go west meant safety; it meant life to people in the awful presence of death. It meant Everything to a people from whom the sea and wind had conspired to take Everything.

So Westwego stands as the perfect example of a great place name, springing as it did from the hearts of a people. To that tortured community, among whose number the native tongue was Malay, Portuguese, French, Spanish or English, Westwego meant Salvation. It is a gusty word, which cannot be inhaled in its pronunciation. It is a cry out! For it was born in the agonizing wake of a howling, murderous wind.

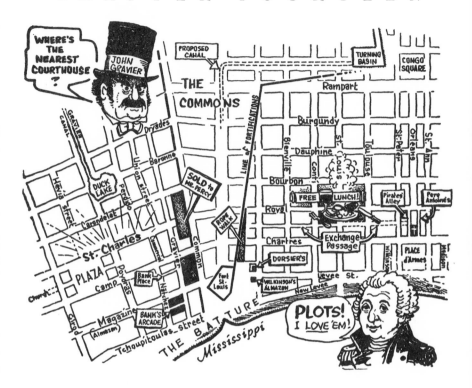

Side Streets and Sidelights

SIDE STREETS AND

SIDELIGHTS . . .

*I*N SPEAKING, you say *Canal* street, with the stress on the prefixed name element. But when you say *Esplanade Avenue,* or *Pontchartrain Boulevard,* both words are spoken with level stress.

Streets are roads in cities. In earliest English usage names given streets were merely descriptive: such as, the Wide street, the High street. And both avenue and boulevard are *additionally* descriptive of streets. An avenue first meant an approach to a place, usually bordered by trees or other ornamentation. In Paris, the Avenue de Grande Armée approaches the Arc de Triomphe. Boulevards, or bulwarks, were once the earthworks in fortifications for artillery pieces. Later, when the need for city fortifications was no more, streets were laid along these boulevards and retained that name. In Paris, the line of streets called the Grandes Boulevards coincides with the ramparts which inclosed the medieval walled city. So avenue and boulevard became terms for extraordinary streets; and it is in this sense that they are applied in the United States, just as are drive, artery, speedway, and expressway.

An alley is also a street, and like avenue and boulevard is of French origin. Alley meant a narrow street. Too narrow for vehicular traffic, an alley was a walkery. Many newer American cities have been planned with service alleys cut through each block, for the convenience of delivery men, garbage collectors, cats, etc., etc. Because this has happened, an alley has come to mean a back street, an unfit address.

But in Louisiana and New Orleans, this does not define an alley. On many an ante-bellum plantation, the cool and shady passages between rows of moss-draped oaks linking the manor houses with the river landings were called, not avenues, but alleys. One such estate, near Donaldsonville, was even formally named Oak Alley for its passageway; and in New Orleans, two of the quaintest side streets are Père Antoine Alley and Pirates' Alley.

Like every other side street in the Vieux Carré, these two did not exist before American domination. As Pauger planned it, Orleans street ended directly behind the cathedral; and remained so until 1831. It was then that Orleans street was stopped at Royal, the cathedral garden formed, and two passages on each side of the whole cathedral property given the names of North Orleans street and South Orleans street. Romanticists and tourist-minded city fathers have more recently changed the two names to Père Antoine Alley and Pirates' Alley.

Antonio de Sedella, for whom one is named, was a Capuchin priest who came to New Orleans in the time of the Spanish governor, Miro. With others of his order, he arrived in 1779 to replace French Capuchins who had died, or left the colony when it ceased to be French. Unquestionably, Sedella was the most able of the group. Three years later he received notice from his superiors back in Spain of his appointment as Commissioner of the Holy Inquisition for New Orleans.

This was disturbing for Sedella. Wherever Spain ruled the Inquisition was, ipso facto, part of the political machinery; and in New Orleans in 1782 Antonio de Sedella was to be it. He dreaded the assignment but orders were orders, and he informed Governor Miro of his appointment and asked for men-at-arms to operate the office. This was disturbing for Miro.

Now comes another of the unexplainable incidents in New Orleans history. Miro didn't say no to Sedella and he didn't say yes. Instead, a few nights later a squad of his soldiers hustled the priest aboard an outgoing ship. So Sedella left, but he returned a few years later, somehow shed of his Inquisition job. He was appointed rector of the St. Louis Church, where his great administrative ability and his zealous and wise conduct of the affairs of the parish brought him prominence in the colony, and endeared him to his French parishioners who affectionately called him Pere Antoine.

The other passage—Pirates' Alley—is named in fanciful recollection of the legendary Jean Lafitte and his motley bank of pirogue-mounted cutthroats, the Baratarians. Lafitte's outfit had no more connection with Pirates' Alley than with the teachings of the church, which the passage flanks on the uptown side. But the name fascinates all visitors.

Madison and Wilkinson streets . . .

In the beginning the two squares above and below Jackson Square (the Place d'Armes) were not privately owned.

Just how Don Andres Almonester y Roxas became the private owner of the choice sites now occupied by the Pontalba buildings is historically hush-hush. Don Andres was a very noble man: a downtown street is called for him, misspelled Almonaster. After the disastrous fire of 1788, he rebuilt the cathedral with his own funds. He also contracted with Governor Carondelet to build a town hall for the colony, a Casa Capitula, to house the Very Illustrious Cabildo—and Carondelet borrowed the money from Almonester to pay him for the job! When a hurricane blew over the Charity Hospital which the sailor, Jean Louis, had founded, Almonester rebuilt that too. With equal generosity he built a chapel for the Ursulines, and was engaged in building the Presbytère when he died.

To a large degree, it might be said of Don Andres that he rebuilt New Orleans, but New Orleans also rebuilt Don Andres. When he came to the city in 1769 he was a penniless Royal Standard Bearer. Whenever a situation or ceremony required somebody to carry the flag, Don Andres Almonester y Roxas was the carrier. He was also a lowly escribano, or notary. He got his big start through the never explained deal between himself and Don Pedro Moris, of the Spanish government, which ended with Almonester owning all the real estate flanking the Place d'Armes to a depth of eighty-four feet on each side. Here he constructed commercial buildings, and from the lush rental came the beginning of the Almonester fortune. Later, his daughter —the fabulous Micaela, Baroness Pontalba—built the present structures on these two sites.

The city continued to own the rear of the two squares, however. And soon after the United States acquired Louisiana, streets were cut through each from Decatur to

Chartres—Wilkinson in 1816 and Madison in 1826. At first Wilkinson was named Jefferson, just as Madison is called for the president of that name. But there already was a Jefferson street in another part of town, so this one was changed to bear the name of General James Wilkinson—and thereby New Orleans' street nomenclature gains added flavor. For certainly General Wilkinson was a flavorful character, and surely his talent for conspiracy was matchless in the history of the Mississippi Valley. A captain in the Revolutionary War, Wilkinson fought with Washington and Benedict Arnold. He acquired a brigadier's star at twenty, but lost it when it was revealed he had plotted with Thomas Conway to oust Washington as commander-in-chief.

After the war Wilkinson settled in Kentucky, and in 1789 he was downriver at New Orleans arranging with Spanish Governor Miro to be agent for Kentucky products in the city for export. Some historians believe he plotted with Miro to make Kentucky a part of Spanish Louisiana; others opine that he and Miro plotted to make an entirely new nation of the Kentucky and Louisiana territories. But all historians join in reporting that he plotted with Aaron Burr who dreamed of empire in the Mississippi Valley—Burr's empire.

Wilkinson also schemed back and forth with Daniel Clark of New Orleans in commercial matters. But regardless of what might be said of the methods of these two men—Wilkinson and Clark—their tireless (and invariably personally profitable) activities in New Orleans and upriver, more than any other factors, stimulated the purchase of the Louisiana territory by the United States.

In 1805, after the Territory of Orleans, which became

the state of Louisiana, was carved from Louisiana, Wilkinson became governor of the vast wilderness remainder. But he soon plotted himself out of this post, and after the War of 1812 he plotted himself out of the army altogether. The last decade of his life was spent in Mexico, happily no doubt, for in these days plots in Mexico were as thick as frijoles.

Besides Wilkinson street, it bears repetition here that the doughty general also accounts for another New Orleans street—Magazine, named for the *magazin* or *almazon* which Miro built to store General Wilkinson's Kentucky products. Magazine street was named for this warehouse.

Dorsier street . . .

Perhaps Eugene Dorsier looked out of the window of his house on New Customhouse street and Levee (now Iberville and Decatur) many a morning at the storage magazine Miro built for Wilkinson's goods. It stood in the batture just across Levee street; and perhaps he even checked incoming and outgoing shipments, for Dorsier's affairs were tied in with Daniel Clark's, and Clark was at least partly incorporated with Wilkinson.

Anyway, there Dorsier lived, and behind the location which was once his house is the alley now called Dorsier street; a bleak and uninteresting little passageway it is too —as bleak as the gleanings about Eugene Dorsier which we get from the historians.

Just down the block from his house sprawled the rope walk of Colonel Sam Davis, who was the general manager of Daniel Clark's operations in New Orleans. And it is a safe assumption that Clark had an interest in this rope walk whose low building extended from Dorsier street almost to Bourbon alongside the crumbling city fortifications. Davis (and Clark?) acquired this rope walk from Elisha Winter, who built it prior to 1790; and as late as 1806 it was still there blocking communication between the city and the Faubourg Ste. Marie.

It seems amiss that there isn't a Rope Walk street in New Orleans. But there is a Dorsier street, named for Eugene Dorsier about whom we can only be sure of two things—he lived there, and he was a witness to Daniel Clark's secret wedding to Zulime Carriere in New York. Maybe even Clark's best man?

Gallatin street was pretty bad . . .

At the same time as Wilkinson and Madison, this street began to appear on maps. Albert Gallatin was Secretary of the Treasury in the cabinet of Jefferson. Of all men, he should have a street or something named for him in Loui· siana, for he had to find ways and means to pay for all the real estate the president had bought from France. For thirty years, beginning in 1840, these were the bawdiest, filthiest, wickedest two blocks in any community anywhere.

Lined with barrel-houses, dance halls, gin mills, and brothels, Gallatin was a king-size successor to the Keelboatmen's Swamp back on Girod street. Historians nod their heads in sad agreement that the harlots of Gallatin established new lows to which human beings might sink, and the male habitués there were more skilled in mayhem, murder, and robbery than ever heretofore known. To this talented crowd of waterfront flotsam and jetsam was added, in 1862, the riff-raff of the North who followed in the wake of conquering Federal armies. Gallatin enjoyed the same immunity from wise and cautious policemen as had The Swamp. It was a lawless street, with Death and Damnation in residence at every address.

Today Gallatin is no longer a street. Buildings on the riverside have disappeared, only the curbs of the farmers' section of the French Market separate it from North Peters and the riverfront docks. Even its name has been altered to French Market Place, and what buildings remain on the opposite side are of remodeled or entirely new construction. Like Sodom and Gomorrah of old, wicked Gallatin street has been erased from the face of the earth.

But across the river in Jefferson Parish, in McDonoughville a street remains called for Secretary Gallatin. He fares better, too, in other sections of the vast Mississippi Valley: counties are named for him in Kentucky and Montana; towns are called Gallatin in Missouri, Illinois, and Tennessee; and in the northwest, a mountain pass, a river, and a national forest bear the name of Albert Gallatin. But for what happened to his good name in New Orleans, the secretary could sue the city!

Ladies never passed along Exchange Passage . . .

For a brief interval this was New Orleans' most important street of commerce. It contributed enormously to American eating habits; and yet—as a street—it died a-borning. Exchange Passage began in 1831, when the Merchants Exchange was built on Royal street with another entrance on the next street, which was created and named for it. But Exchange Passage was not wholly concerned with the affairs of the Merchants Exchange. It went to other exchanges . . . and to other places!

Bear in mind in 1831 the Creoles in the Vieux Carré

held the initiative over the impudent Kaintocks across Canal street. It was not until 1835 that the municipalities were divided, and the Americans began to get an even break in the city council, and, soon afterwards, more than their share of the commercial breaks.

With a slight jog at Iberville street, Exchange Passage sliced through the next three squares to the main entrance of the City Exchange, domiciled in the St. Louis Hotel which was built in 1835. Nearby, at the Chartres corner, was the exchange and coffee shop of Pierre Maspero. Historians also speak of Hewlett's exchange in the same immediate neighborhood, and exactly at the corner of St. Louis street and Exchange Passage was the establishment of an Englishman who sold a strange new-fangled beverage called beer. For a long time this was the only place in New Orleans where the sudsy nectar was available. There, also, was the cockpit where Charles Hicks staged hotly contested cockfights; and, of course, the bar in the St. Louis Hotel was the city's finest.

It is unbelievable that Exchange Passage would ever be able to pull itself away from so fascinating an intersection, and continue in a businesslike manner to the Cabildo. This was the city hall of the First Municipality, where Creole businessmen must go to register sales, etc. and otherwise consummate commercial transaction. When it did continue, its route was unique. From St. Louis street, Exchange Passage went through the lobby (and no doubt also the bar) of the St. Louis Hotel, out the back into the Improvement Bank (later Citizens Bank), and through the bank's front door on Toulouse street. From here to the next street, St. Peter, was a difficult way for the Creole businessmen. Some historians surmise that they hopped fences and otherwise proceeded through the center of this block. There was much talk about the First Municipality buying property and clearing a right-of-way for Exchange Passage to St. Peter street, but it is evident this never happened. Exchange Passage was never more than a dotted line on maps between Toulouse and St. Peter, and following a dotted line must have been exceedingly trying for the businessmen—especially after all the diversions on St. Louis street. However, the First Municipality did move back the fence of the prison yard behind the Cabildo for Exchange Passage from St. Peter to Orleans (or Pirates') Alley. It still exists, now called Cabildo Alley.

There are those who will ask why these Creole businessmen didn't walk down to Chartres street and thence to the Cabildo? Such a question can only come from sources unacquainted with Creole businessmen (vintage of the 1830's), and unacquainted with the kind of traffic encountered on Chartres street—and also on Royal street on the opposite side of Exchange Passage.

Chartres and Royal were the two great shopping streets of the First Municipality. Women were there! Women buying bonnets and parasols and lace and calico, etc., etc. Women are wonderful, the men of business reasoned, but they didn't mix with business. Exchange Passage was a stag street hemmed in by petticoats.

Even getting lunch was a problem. But this was a problem most emphatically licked by M. Philippe Alvarez, manager of the St. Louis Hotel Bar in 1837. From the genius of Alvarez came the free lunch! The real business in the exchanges—the auctioneering—took place between the hours of noon and three o'clock. There simply wasn't time to stop at a bar, go home for lunch, and get back to business. In desperation, many businessmen gave up lunch. Others gave up business. Alvarez's plan—to give free lunch to all who stopped in the St. Louis Bar for a toddy—saved many a business career.

Other bars quickly took up the idea, and soon each was seeking to outdo the others in the excellence of its free lunch. From Exchange Passage, from New Orleans, the free lunch spread all over the United States, and continued as an American institution until prohibition. After the repeal of the 18th Amendment, and the bars reopened, it was without that wonderful invention of Philippe Alvarez —free lunch.

Today, Exchange Passage—rechristened Exchange Place —runs three blocks from Canal to Conti. The building which once housed the Merchants Exchange, and which gave the street its name, still exists. It's a restaurant, with its service entrance on Exchange Place. Practically every other building in the first block is a bar!

The other two blocks are narrower and without accommodations for vehicular traffic. They are quiet now, and seem a little sad about the battle for commercial superiority which the Creole businessmen fought and lost along its way. In fact, even the free lunch it gave the nation is lost too.

St. Charles street was No. 1 . . .

Rome wasn't built in a day. Neither was the American Section of New Orleans. It took the Americans seventeen years to make a world famous community of the Faubourg Ste. Marie, which Bertrand Gravier had inherited from his wife's first husband. And then St. Charles street was its lifeline.

In 1836 the first great American hotel, named for and located on St. Charles street opened; two years later James H. Caldwell rang up the curtain on the most palatial theater in America, also named St. Charles and located on that street. These two edifices just about made every other street in the world a side street to St. Charles.

And it was a gay, bright, and lively street, with an air of exciting bohemianism about it. Between Canal street and Hevia (now Lafayette) there were forty-five bars, counting the great marble octagonal temple of hot toddies in the St. Charles Hotel. This spa measured seventy feet in diameter. There were rooming houses, too, on the upper floors of the buildings to supplement the sleeping accommodations of the St. Charles Hotel, and the Verandah just across the street from it. And to supplement the free lunches in the bars, there were also restaurants. Historians mention few other types of business on the street, except that of an exceedingly high-minded character who opened a library. Soon facing bankruptcy, this character (who was a business-man, after all) shifted some bookcases and put in a sixty-foot bar. After this addition the library prospered. St. Charles was that kind of a street in 1837.

But St. Charles almost failed to survive and realize this glittering destiny, following its dedication to public use, as a street, by Bertrand Gravier in 1788.

Presumably, according to the Common Law of dedication, by which method all New Orleans streets have originated, Gravier had divested himself of ownership of the street as completely as if he had made a direct sale or donation of the street to the public. Nevertheless, Gravier sold a block of St. Charles street!

Following the fire of 1788, when Bertrand Gravier and

his wife subdivided their faubourg into squares and lots, they retained as their place of residence the square bounded by Magazine, Gravier, Camp and the commons —or Common street, as it later became. Their house faced Magazine, and in the rear of their plot were the huts of their Negro slaves.

Not long after the subdivision, Gravier sold the two squares behind the one he occupied to Pierre Percy—two squares bounded by Gravier and Common, and including St. Charles street through this block! Twelve years later, the city council voted to pay Mr. Percy $4,000 to recut St. Charles street through his property, then a flourishing vegetable garden.

The Graviers were always doing things like this, including John Gravier who acquired the whole faubourg— minus 107 lots sold—when Bertrand and his wife died. It was John who tried long and desperately to get back the public place (later named Lafayette Square) which Bertrand had dedicated as a plaza to adorn the suburb. John was thrown out of the Spanish Tribunal and the American courts three times during nine years of litigation. The city's rights to the square were finally upheld in 1822 by the Louisiana Supreme Court, which decided that the case had acquired the force and authority of res adjudica; that is, the case rested as already judged and Gravier's claim was null and void. The square was named Lafayette in 1824, following the French general's visit to New Orleans. At about the same time, two strips were shaved off its north and south sides for streets, and given the factual names they still bear—North and South.

The plain truth is that John Gravier loved to go to court. Historians count up that he was either suing or being sued twenty-two times in nineteen consecutive years, a local record only topped by Myra Clark Gaines. But John Gravier was not involved in a lengthy litigation concerning Poydras street at Baronne.

Poydras is wider beyond Baronne, because out there Poydras was designed to accommodate the Gravier Canal in its middle. This canal, never more than a sluggish crawfish ditch, was decked out with a turning basin, popularly called Duck Lake in Spanish days.

The basin's boundaries, and the public places which were adjuncts to it, included the Baronne and Poydras intersection as far in as Carroll street, and the two small squares bounded by Carroll, Perdido and Penn. In time this area became the property of the New Orleans and Carrollton Railroad, which permitted the city to recut Baronne street through the then filled in basin. Here was another instance where Bertrand Gravier had originally dedicated a street (Baronne) , and then sold a block of it!

The N. O. & C. R. R. used the two squares on Baronne, between Poydras and Perdido, for its New Orleans terminal; and when steam trains were discontinued for mule pulled cars (an improvement?) the cars were parked on the Carroll street side and the mule pen was on the Penn street side. Although Penn street is actually named in honor of Davidson B. Penn, the intrepid lieutenant governor who led in the uprising of the White League on September 14, 1874, it also serves to recall that here was the mule pen for N. O. & C. R. R. mules off duty. Carroll street is named in honor of John Carroll, a city policeman who was killed in line of duty at the L. & N. station in 1908. Previous names for these two streets were East and West.

Side Street and Sidelights . . .

Thomas Banks, who blew up and burst . . .

One of the heaviest investors in the American Section, and one of the least known "city fathers" of New Orleans was this enterprising Englishman. Following his arrival in the city in 1814, Banks worked as a day laborer until he had acquired sufficient funds to open a sailors' boarding house on the riverfront. He operated this salty establishment for twenty years. By then he had sufficient funds to build the City Hotel on the corner of Camp and Common streets where the International Trade Mart now stands. Banks speculated heavily in real estate, and owned much of it in the American section, including the entire square bounded by Magazine, Gravier, Tchoupitoulas, and Natchez. On this site, in 1833, he engaged Zimpel to build the city's first office building.

Called Banks Arcade, it was for years the largest building in the city—three stories high, and a block long on Magazine, with main entrances on both Gravier and Natchez into a glass covered arcade, which cut the building exactly in half and gave it its name. Banks' tenants included the St. James Hotel, a newspaper, an exchange, a restaurant, a barber shop, and—well, guide books of the time boasted that 5,000 people could use the building at one time for various purposes. Pretty good for 1835.

And among the things for which Banks Arcade was used was the plotting of the Texas revolution; and many another filibustering expedition into Spanish America was dreamed up during the office hours of the Arcade's heyday.

But alas for speculating Thomas Banks. He was caught short in the Panic of 1837. In 1842 he went bankrupt, and lived the last fourteen years of his life amid the scenes of his great achievements in retirement and poverty. Arcade

Place, now the address of the Board of Trade, is the only street anywhere which has been converted from the corridor of an office building.

Also block-long Picayune Place was originally called Banks Place for Thomas Banks. It was changed to Picayune when *The Picayune,* fore-runner of *The Times-Picayune,* was located on Camp street with its busy back door on this street. But back-of-town, lateralling off of Tulane Avenue, is another street named for Thomas Banks, which continues to be so called.

Commercial and Natchez—but don't call 'em alleys! . . .

These two narrow streets (Commercial is a walkery) are in the heart of the business district, once the American Section. Because they were narrow, Orleanians acquired the habit of calling them alleys—much to the noisy indignation of certain businessmen located there. As a matter of fact, they have never been officially designated as alleys, and the long-time habit of so calling them is fading under the glare of the outraged executives, who inhabit the streets during the business day. Natchez street is named for the Mississippi river city, and Commercial Place recalls the Commercial Exchange which stood on the corner of Perdido and St. Charles streets.

Perdido and Union—the Frerets fathered both . . .

Approaching from the river, Commercial is almost a continuation of Natchez at Camp street; and at St. Charles, Perdido and Union vie for the privilege of being the continuation of Commercial.

Perdido . . . that this street was always getting lost and was so named, is the legend. But that isn't the only unusual thing about Perdido street. It isn't altogether clear when it was first found either! As its Spanish name indicates, the street predates American domination in 1803. It was first cut from the swamp in as far as Carondelet, and probably was so designated by Bertrand Gravier. But the way that man would dedicate a street and then sell a strip of it gives every indication that poor Perdido may well have gotten just as lost on Gravier's maps as it is alleged to have gotten in Gravier's swamps.

It was the Freret brothers—William and James—who extended Perdido to St. Charles and securely anchored it there. The Frerets operated the first large industry in the American Section. Had not their huge cotton press occupied nearly two blocks on St. Charles, between Poydras and Gravier, there would probably have been room for more than the forty-five bars on that thirsty thoroughfare. In 1813 William Freret received permission from the city council to cut another street through his property. This was Union, so called because it united St. Charles and Dryades streets. William Freret later became mayor, and for him uptown Freret street is named.

The Show is over on Varieties Alley . . .

This convenient little "short-cut" passageway connecting Gravier and Common streets, between Carondelet and Baronne, retains little evidence of its former distinction. It is the only street in the city which was created to accommodate the theater crowds, for on the corner of Varieties Alley and Gravier was the well-known and well-patronized Varieties Theater. Manager of the Varieties, and also player of many roles there, was Tom Placide, brother of James H. Caldwell's beloved Jane. Caldwell, himself, had a large interest in the theater, but he was never openly identified with its operation, which commenced in 1849.

Church is out on Church street . . .

More recently, but just as completely as Varieties Alley, this street has lost its identifying landmark. It has also lost part of its length. In 1834, when the First Presbyterian Church was built on Lafayette Square alongside St. Mary street, that street soon acquired the name of Church. Later the street was extended through the next block to Julia. But in 1938, the church moved uptown, and sold its site to the U. S. government. The government also bought Church street, between the square and Girod street, from the city; and the huge Federal Building now occupies both as part of its broad frontage on Lafayette Square. So . . . one block of Church street remains, with the part of the street which acquired its name sold to the government, and the church from which the name was acquired moved five miles uptown. Church street is unquestionably the most side-tracked side street in New Orleans.

Perrilliat and Hevia—they lived there . . .

Just as Gravier, Poydras, Girod, and Julia streets bear the names of those who were among the first to live in or invest in the Faubourg Ste. Marie—so, too, does Perrilliat street. Francois Perrilliat fished in the Gravier Canal as a boy, and was a prominent trader in his adult years. Back on the street now named for him were his warehouses. Another pioneer into the section was Augustine Garcia Hevia. The original name of Lafayette street was Hevia, and it was still called so by oldsters as late as 1900.

The batture was a beachhead . . .

In the chapter, "Creole vs. Kaintock—Round Two," mention has already been made of the batture. The meandering, mischievous Mississippi River, in its journey to the gulf, frequently chips off one side of its bank and deposits additional bank on the opposite side. The pieces it took away never seem to have caused so much trouble as the pieces it puts back—and none ever caused so much long drawn out trouble as the piece it put at the riverfront of Gravier's Faubourg Ste. Marie, the American Section of New Orleans.

It was the celebrated and argumentative lawyer, Edward Livingston, who made this piece of land so unpeaceful for so long. Lawyer Livingston was the younger brother of Robert Livingston who had dickered with Napoleon for the purchase of Louisiana, and who had been a partner with Robert Fulton in his river steamboat pioneering. When he arrived in New Orleans in 1803, Edward Livingston was broke, and casting about in this new land of opportunity for quick means to restore his fortune, he obtained —guess who?—John Gravier for a client!

In Livingston's opinion, Gravier owned the batture; and Gravier was ready and willing to agree heartily with anybody who believed that he owned anything. Practically everybody else in New Orleans disagreed with them; the batture had long been used as a public place, convenient for shipping, and a bountiful supply of free river sand filling. Of course, Gravier had fenced off a section of the batture (between Julia and St. Joseph), but Gravier was the sort of guy, who—given enough barbed wire—would fence off the Garden of Eden for himself. Even so, Livingston remained convinced that Gravier's claim to the batture before his faubourg was good, and himself purchased from Gravier that section of the batture from Julia to Common street. He paid $80,000 for it. In Edward Livingston, John Gravier had the kind of lawyer every client dreams of!

But Livingston never got possession of his property. Thousands of indignant citizens joined in the riots which ensued when he tried to fence in his beachhead. Litigation, set in motion by Livingston, continued long years after the lawyer (Livingston), his client (Gravier), and the principal target of all this legal warring (Thomas Jefferson) had all died.

The rights of the city were ultimately upheld, and gradually streets through the batture began to appear on maps. The Faubourg Ste. Marie, however, was not the only section of the city with a batture. The river had also deposited lagniappe land before the Vieux Carré, and alongside Tchoupitoulas street as far up as Felicity. Gravier's batture was distinguished because it was the largest, and because it was disputed; but the first batture streets came from below Canal street.

Decatur street was originally called Levee. As this name implies, here was the levee; and all land now on the riverside of Decatur, once Levee, is alluvial. Prior to 1815, a street was dedicated which lateralled off Levee at Conti into the batture, and named New Levee. Later, this same street was continued above Canal street, through the disputed batture, and all the way up to Felicity.

In themselves, names of streets in the batture contribute little to New Orleans' fanciful street nomenclature. Like

New Levee—which, incidentally, has been changed to North and South Peters—most seem preoccupied with their location on the busy waterfront, such as, Front street, Commerce street, and Water street. Civil War mariners called this last Wide Water street, because then it was the last street between the buildings and the water's edge, some distance away across the open wharves. Since then Delta street has been inserted between Water street and the water.

Other batture streets are named for a mayor, Crossman; a governor, Wells; a good friend of the city, Henry Clay; and a good friend of the river, Robert Fulton. Another is called Clinton . . . this block long street behind the Customhouse is either named for De Witt Clinton or his uncle, George Clinton—celebrated New York politicians —or Sir Henry Clinton of the Coldstream Guards. Both De Witt and George fought in a Revolutionary battle against Sir Henry—maybe to decide for whom this block long street is named? But the battle was indecisive.

St. Mary's Market had an air . . .

Also in the batture was the American counterpart to the French Market, and named for the faubourg, St. Mary. Unlike the French Market, whose first venders were Indian hunters and fishermen and German farmers from Des Allemands, and whose more recent merchants are predominantly Italian, the St. Mary's Market was Irish for all its eighty-six years. It began just when Irish immigration to New Orleans was heaviest, and it was placed just where most of the Irish settled.

In 1836 two new streets were cut through a square of

ground from Tchoupitoulas to New Levee (South Peters), between Howard and St. Joseph, and the market was built between them. The two new streets were named North Market and South Market. There on the downtown edge of the Irish Channel, St. Mary's Market built up one of the important shopping sections of its day. More than one successful merchant got his start around St. Mary's, then moved to Canal street. Spokesmen for the neighborhood declare that the Diamond Hotel was the city's first hostelry. It stood across Tchoupitoulas street from the market, and in 1948 the building still stood there.

But just as Gallatin street, near the French Market, went wicked, so did St. Mary's neighborhood have its black sheep. Actually, in 1836, this section had not yet quieted down from the roughhouse routine which the keelboatmen had inaugurated there, and the new residents—Irishmen—were not of a racial group notable for quiet and peaceful ways. Happy-go-lucky hoodlums banded into organizations with such picturesque names as: the St. Mary Market Gang, the Shot Tower Gang, the Crowbar Gang, and others. Those who opposed them were neither happy nor lucky; it was a tough precinct for policemen, and more than one was killed.

Earlier, the residents in the faubourgs of Nuns and Lafayette had sought sanctuary in the creation of a new parish for protection from keelboatmen's pranks. In the newspapers of 1824, petitioning for the new parish, these residents complain of the "lack of protection from city policemen." The new parish was organized the following year, and given the name of Jefferson! So, between the city of Lafayette—first capital of Jefferson—and the business section of the St. Mary's Market, the violence of the Irish Channel was contained and, in time, tamed. The market, itself, was closed in 1922. North Market street and South Market street are now North and South Diamond streets; and the site of the market is a parkway.

CHAPTER FIFTEEN

"Quartée red beans, quartée rice,
Little piece of salt meat to make it taste nice,
Lend me the paper, and tell me the time;
When papa passes by, he'll pay you the dime"

...and Lagniappe

...AND LAGNIAPPE

ONCE—a very long time ago, it seems—neighborly Creole merchants presented each customer some trifling gift after a sale. It was something extra, a gratuity, a way they had of thanking customers for their trade. And the name for it was lagniappe.

What a pity no street name perpetuates this curious name for this wonderful custom. For now efficient chain stores and super markets have crowded out the neighborhood corner groceries and notion nooks, and with their disappearance lagniappe has also disappeared. In fact, many of the newer generation of Orleanians no longer know the meaning of the word. And lagniappe isn't in all dictionaries.

The romantic story of New Orleans, which the street names have to tell, is told.

Physical growth of the city since the time of World War II is similar to any other American community. Naming new streets has become a business-like function—usually carefully planned with the post office supervisor of mail deliveries.

So this is an old story, and rightly entitled to revive an old custom. It is, then, as lagniappe that these last few pages are included with the story of the street names. Unrelated episodes they are, sometimes trifling, sometimes pertinent —such as the account of Allan d'Hemicourt and Louis Pilié, authors of the official map of New Orleans.

On June 4, 1855, the *Daily Picayune* reported that Jules Allan d'Hemicourt had been employed by the Council to make a plan of city property at a cost of $30,000. Due to overspeculations and foreclosures following financial panics, much of the back-of-town was not privately owned and was undeveloped, and the various faubourgs were as orderly islands in a wilderness of cypress woods, swamps, and cane brakes. It was d'Hemicourt's problem to make an integrated unit of all this, a master plan of the city.

Louis Pilié (his name is pronounced pee-lee-a) joined d'Hemicourt in the months-long task of surveying and triangulating the area into city squares. The work of plotting a map was entrusted to Pilié, which he finished in a year and sent to Paris for engraving.

Whether d'Hemicourt and Pilié were ever paid by the city is not clear. However, in 1856 a circular was printed and circulated by them petitioning the general public to subscribe for copies of "a map showing the numbers of all the squares within the city limits, and also within Jefferson and Algiers and Metairie." The map was described as drawn to the scale of one ten thousandth of an inch, and the price was advertised $25.

No map was more ill-fated.

The copy sent to Paris was lost at sea. War between the North and South broke out and nobody was interested in maps of New Orleans—excepting, maybe, the high command of the Yankee armies. Also, d'Hemicourt died, and his son, who had worked with the partners, quarreled and severed relations with Pilié.

Years passed. Then one day there turned up in the city another copy of this map, five times larger than the first, drawn on 48 sheets of eggshell paper with black and red ink. Although the map was unsigned, it appeared to duplicate the information of the shipwrecked first map and contained exceedingly valuable data. After passing through many hands, the city finally bought this map from a colonel of dragoons who was stuck with it as security for an unpaid loan of $250. The colonel was glad to let the city have all 48 sheets for $100 cash. So, thirty-seven years after the project had been authorized, the city got possession of its official map of itself. It is the basis of all maps since drawn of New Orleans.

Nobody will ever know how many streets d'Hemicourt and Pilié gave names, as they crisscrossed the vacant lands of the back-of-town with new streets. We can be sure of the ones they named for two real estate speculators, Alex Baudin and Thomas Banks. (Banks died while the survey was in progress.) And we can also be sure of one named for d'Hemicourt too. None was named for Pilié. Perhaps the oddest name which can be attributed to these two surveyors is Lapeyrouse; but its explanation is simple, John B. Lapeyrouse, a goldsmith, lived in the vicinity of this street.

Hundreds of street names in New Orleans have been changed. With each owner subdividing his property and naming streets, it can readily be seen what happened when the faubourgs all grew together. Many a street had different names for parts of its length: such as Rampart, which was called—in parts—Love, Delphina, St. Nicholas, St. Denis, Circus, Hercules, and Mobile Landing. There were many duplications too: such as, a half dozen Napoleon streets, and numerous others all named for George Washington, St. John the Baptist, General Lafayette, or Henry Clay—the most popular names for streets.

Three major efforts were made to remedy this condition. Ordinances, passed in 1852, 1894, and 1932, changed scores of street names—and more than one amusing incident has resulted. For instance, there is still a Robin Street Wharf at the foot of Euterpe street, which used to be named (nearest the river) for Robin Delogny. And there is a Robin street now, miles away from the wharf and named for the bird!

It was the ordinance of 1894 which changed all the numbered streets of Carrollton to the names of trees, which they still bear. This ordinance also changed Port street to Moss —so trees and moss entered the street nomenclature together.

Commissions appointed by the mayor to change street names know they have a thankless job, they are certain they will displease more people than they can please, and are resigned to the fact that older people are going to continue stubbornly to call streets their original names until they breathe their last.

Among those displeased by changes in street names are the historians, who raise several interesting points. In 1932, the changers sought to name a projection of Scott street, Ivanhoe street. The historians pointed out that Scott street is named for General Winfield Scott and not Sir Walter. A like instance was a suggestion that Josephine Alley, downtown, be changed to Beauharnais Alley. The changers hopefully explained how historically relative this would be, as Beauharnais was Josephine Bonaparte's first husband, who was guillotined during the Reign of Terror. But Josephine Alley wasn't named for Napoleon's (and Beauharnais') Josephine, but for a neighborhood personality; and was ultimately changed to Rosalie Alley—another neighborhood personality.

Street name changers also got historically lost on winding Crete street—an eight block long thoroughfare between the Jockey Club Racetrack and Ursulines street. Crete is in the ancient Faubourg St. John, subdivided for Daniel Clark by Lafon in 1809. And Crete street is even older than this.

Here's how it happened: just as Bayou Metairie had ridges or crests (crête in French) on both sides of it, the most pronounced of which became Metairie Ridge Road, so, too, did Bayou Sauvage have its ridges. Both Bayous Metairie and Sauvage were originally one and the same stream—the Supicatcha, or Mudfish River, of the Choctaws. The ridge on the right bank of Bayou Sauvage became Gentilly Road, and the crest on the opposite—left—bank was popularly called *La Crête* Road. Once it ran for some distance along the bayou in the direction of Chef Menteur.

In 1932 a commission of street name changers sought to correct some of the confusion encountered by seven streets which cross Canal, between Broad and Jefferson Davis, and venture downtown into the Faubourg St. John. A glance at any city map will show how the streets in this section run in different alignment from all other streets around them. Streets as well as people get lost in the Faubourg St. John, and these seven did. All of them end up differently; and what is more unusual, two which disappear in the faubourg miraculously reappear on the other side of it, beyond Gentilly Road! The commissioners went into a huddle over this and decided that such conduct upon the part of Gayoso and Dupre—they were the two streets which faded out and then faded in—made them entirely different streets. So they gave them different names beyond Gentilly Road; Romulus and Theseus they would be.

Then for some unexplainable reason the commission decided to explain why they had selected Theseus as the name of the reappeared section of Dupré. This street, they pointed out, was just across Gentilly Road from Crete street, and it would be both historically and classically appropriate to call it Theseus after the celebrated hero of Crete. Theseus was the Greek hatchet boy who slew the Minotaur, a disagreeable (and hungry) mythological monster of the island of Crete who had to be served regular feedings of Athenian youths and virgins—or else.

It is equally unexplainable how the historians won their point here. But neither Gayoso nor Dupre was changed as recommended; and Crete street—*La Crête* Road—continues to recall the *crête* or ridge, of Bayou Sauvage.

Colapissa is another street which dips far back into regional history for its name. This Carrollton street was little known until the Illinois Central Railroad built tracks into town along its way; soon everybody knew where Colapissa was and wondered what it was.

Perhaps when Zimpel was laying out Carrollton the last man of the Colapissa tribe of the Choctaw Nation walked by, or lived near-by. It's hard to believe there could have been more than one, for the Colapissas were an ancient clan, whose name in Choctaw means "see-people, sentinels, or spies." Their camp, in the days of Choctaw glory was on the eastern fringe of the tribal domain, on the Teleatcha or Rock River whose name Penicaut changed to Pearl River when he mistook the rocks there for pearls. The Colapissas spread the warning among the other tribes when enemy war parties invaded Choctaw country—or anyway they were supposed to.

For the same reason that Customhouse street was changed to Iberville, South Rampart street—from St. Andrew to Nashville—became Danneel. Customhouse ran through the wicked red light district of Storyville and was thus contaminated. There were also wicked goings-on along some downtown sections of Rampart street in the year 1910. People who lived further up the street didn't like the name of Rampart for an address. So on February 1, 1910, by city ordinance, Rampart became Danneel above St. Andrew street.

Rudolph Danneel was a strange, quiet fellow who grew to manhood during the Reconstruction Era. Nothing ever happened to Danneel, not even marriage. He inherited his father's brokerage business, and lived alone busily plying his hobby of evenings, which was setting poetry he liked to music. Perhaps it is just as well that he lived alone.

He bequeathed a square of ground to the city when he died, and the grateful municipality has named a school and this street for Rudolph Danneel. But, who knows? had there not been so much cutting up on downtown Rampart street, Danneel memorials would have been confined to a school.

Today, when one motors from one end of New Orleans to the other, the street will at regular intervals turn sharply. An obvious reason for this is the bending river to which the street must conform. But it is also interesting to recollect that each such turn encountered indicated that you are crossing from one colonial plantation to another —privately owned tracts all of which today comprise the city of New Orleans. As an example along Claiborne Avenue (both South and North) turns at Lowerline, Upperline, Delachaise, Felicity, St. Bernard and Almonaster all indicate ancient property lines.

Further back from the river, particularly in the uptown section, turns are more frequent and more abrupt. Certain streets there give the appearance of not knowing where to go, and infrequent visitors in these neighborhoods will quickly find themselves in a similar dilemma.

These various plantations, or faubourgs, developed at different times, and they did not always knit together smoothly. Nowhere is this better illustrated than in the case of North Rampart and St. Claude. While the latter is, in reality, a continuation of the old street built on the ramparts, the two streets do not connect! One block before Rampart meets St. Claude, it turns to its right and runs alongside St. Claude—one block nearer the river—all the way to the city limits. And St. Claude, coming from the other way, also turns right before meeting Rampart, and continues alongside that street as far as the Auditorium. McShane street—named for a mayor—connects these two streets which refuse to meet.

From the beginning, as John Law started it in the Vieux Carré, personalities have strongly influenced New Orleans street names. Two and a half centuries of interesting people have passed across the New Orleans scene, leaving their stories indexed in the street nomenclature. There are stories of great men who did little things: such as Placide Louis Chapelle, Archbishop of New Orleans and apostolic delegate to Cuba, Porto Rico and the Philippine Islands, who was charged with the reorganization of the Catholic Church in these far-flung regions after the Spanish American War. But he found time to assist the Dominicans in establishing a chapel in Lakeview, and Chapelle street there is named for him.

Paul Morphy street recalls a little man who became great while yet a beardless boy. At least in the eyes of chess players the world over this Creole youth forever ranks as an all-time great. He retired from match play at twenty-two for lack of competition, and died some years later when he stepped into a cold bath after a hot walk—probably the only wrong move Paul Morphy ever made.

And perhaps the Chevrolet of Joseph Alfred Blythe belongs among the personalities which have influenced street names? Blythe, a professional promoter of subdivisions, was often confronted with the problem of naming streets; and, as has always been the case since the time of John Law, sought street names which would stimulate settlement. Shortly after World War I, Blythe had a new subdivision ready for street names, a downtown tract adjoining the prospering suburb of Gentilly Terrace. After many conferences with his associates, names of automobiles— then becoming low priced and popular—were suggested. Blythe agreed to this, with one exception . . . none would be named Chevrolet, because Mr. Blythe's automobile of that name was giving him trouble at the time!

So streets were given names of all the autos they could think of, and in this section just below Peoples Avenue streets are called Ford, Velie, Buick, Stutz, Packard, Lincoln, and Cadillac. And Mr. Blythe got even with his obstinate automobile—no street was called for the popular Chevrolet.

And as for lagniappe . . . in the city, with its fifteen hundred street names, the New Orleans Post Office in 1948 was still operating six RFD routes!

Surely, to any story of city streets RFD routes are something extra . . . or *lagniappe!*

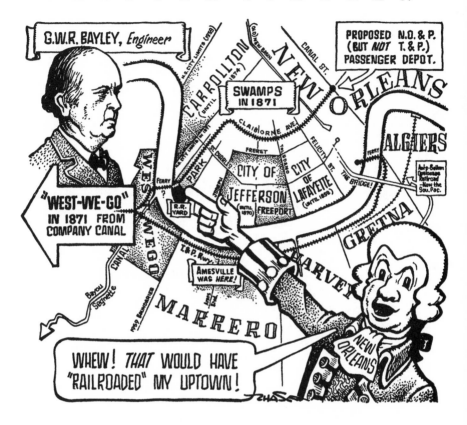

Grade-Crossings,
River-Crossings –
and
Double-Crossings

GRADE-CROSSINGS,

RIVER-CROSSINGS

— AND DOUBLE-

CROSSINGS

*T*EN YEARS AGO, when I wrote this book, I thought I was through with the streets of New Orleans.

Then, almost immediately, more began to happen to the streets and the city than during any other decade since 1718, when Bienville ordered dePailloux and his eighty bootleggers (see page 21) to clear away the cypress thick‑ ets along the riverbank for the streets of a settlement.

Just look at New Orleans! Twenty-two grade separations costing $27,345,840.81 have been built on streets all over town, allowing traffic to move over or under pokey freight trains on crossing railroad tracks. There are even interchanges, which from passing airliners look for all the world like giant forkfuls of spaghetti dropped upon the ground, and to local motorists unused to such things, no less confusing.

Then there's a new Union Passenger Terminal. Not since 1832, when the second railroad in the United States, the *Pontchartrain,* left its Elysian Fields terminal at the river for its inaugural trip to the lake, have *all* the city's railroads been able to leave from one terminal to go their appointed ways. Incidentally, this new terminal that was opened to the public in 1954 cost two million dollars more than the entire capital stock of the *Pontchartrain Railroad* when it was chartered 124 leargs earlier.

To accommodate nearly three times as many automobiles as there were ten years ago, the longest auto bridge in the world has been built across the lake to Mandeville. Another record-breaking bridge rises into the skyline at Thalia street to span the river. Add to this some twenty new subdivisions, all with new streets. Add, too, the 32,000-acre Faubourg de Montluzin. Located downtown below Paris Road and extending to Chef Menteur, Faubourg de Montluzin comprises one fourth of the land area of the corporate city, and in 1949 most of it was swamps. Nevertheless, New Orleans East, Inc.—a private company—was pushing ahead with plans to subdivide it all, with miles and miles of new streets and new street names. In scope, this ambitious project amounts to adding to the settled area of the city a settlement the size of Baton Rouge.

But speaking of swamps, back in 1834 the region just behind North Rampart street alongside the Poydras canal was a cypress swamp, so unsuitable for human habitation that Orleanians called it the "quarter of the damned". There it was that old John Gravier died in a shanty Etienne Carriby had permitted him to occupy rent-free. In the years that followed, this region never developed into much more than a disreputable neighborhood. Then, in 1953, the city cleared away eleven acres of slums and created a Civic Center, with a new city hall, two new court houses, a state office building and a most modern public library. These five new buildings are arranged around a landscaped plaza named Duncan, in memory of Brooke Duncan, the city planner who conceived this happy ending for the ante-bellum "quarter of the damned". John Gravier's shanty was on South Liberty street just off Poydras, about where the elevators in the new city hall are now located! In the not too distant future, the transformation of swampy Faubourg de Montluzin will probably be no less remarkable.

In the Civic Center-Union Station neighborhood, new wide streets have been carved that streak off into many directions. Major streets they call them; and like Roman roads of old they tolerate no obstructions in their arrow-straight forward progress to outlying regions. Many an old street with its old name, unhappily in the path of one of these modern major streets, has been hacked into, or chopped apart and sometimes has completely disappeared. Frequently, I have been introduced as an expert on New Orleans streets, but in recent years more than once I have become hopelessly lost in the new arrangement of things. This was particularly embarrassing that morning I drove out Palm street to make a talk about streets at Country Day School. I was late for the speech, because something happened to Palm street as I knew it, and I ended up on the approach to the Huey P. Long Bridge. It is difficult for an expert to explain a thing like this.

Nothing like what has happened to the streets of New Orleans has ever happened before, until I wrote this book about them. Certainly, not in any ten year period. I feel that the city fathers and the city planners have double-crossed me.

On the other hand, maybe I would never have become lost on Palm street, and been made into a shame-faced "expert", if this book hadn't double-crossed me first. As it says on page ix, for more than a hundred times I had been called upon to make talks and speeches about New Orleans streets. For as good a reason as any I wrote the book to shut me up. In this respect, *Frenchmen, Desire, Good Children* proved a disappointment. For every speech I made before the book, I made two more after its publication. Such speeches, I have learned, are called book reviews; and there is no easy escape from them by authors. Even before the book was put on sale, I had thirty-two reviews scheduled.

In other respects, however, the book fared well. All the thousands of copies were sold, and this is a comfort to a writer exceeded only by the publisher's satisfaction in not having to eat the things. Also, by those whose judgments and opinions I respect, the book was declared worthwhile; and the Louisiana Library Association even gave it an award. "We believe it to be the most distinguished book on Louisiana published during 1949," said the certificate they gave me. It was very nice of the librarians to do this, especially after the way I'm always bothering them—with questions, that is.

After the book was out for awhile, and I was about 47% through reviewing it, certain inaccuracies were called to my attention from time to time by observing and informing friends of mine. "You've misspelled one of Louis XIV's girl friend's name," one of them pointed out. Another explained that I had the Battle of New Orleans underway after the Battle of Waterloo, which he declared bluntly raised more hell with history than Sherman declared war to be in the first place. A descendant of General Francis T. Nicholls telephoned to call me names for calling his great grandfather an Irish-American near the bottom of page 61. "He was a Creole," the man said over the phone and through his teeth, which isn't easy. Then, there was that lady at the Kessels' cocktail party. Why did I spell the name of Judge George Trauth on page 194 with an "o", she demanded to know, backing me against the wall. With an "o" you spell the trout that is a fish, she informed me. The judge's name is spelled Trauth with an "a", and he signed it that way on all of those 18,-985 marriage licenses to prove it, she added testily.

I'm sorry about changing the name of the girl friend of Louis XIV. But, after all, that's more than Louis did for her. In the case of the Battles of New Orleans and Waterloo, I was only six months wrong on page 155 having the "veterans of Waterloo" storming Jackson's line at Chalmette. For Pakenham to have sent his hapless troopers against such firepower on that January morning in 1815 was, I suggest, a far more serious military miscalculation. My critical friend, I must add, has rejected this excuse.

I shall always remember the day Lou Milliner came over from the Associated Press. "Where is Prieur street that I live on?" Lou wanted to know, waving his copy of this book. He certainly had a justifiable complaint, and a good excuse not to go home. His street, the one named for Denis Prieur, mayor of the city during the formative years of the American Section, was missing from page 180, where it belonged between Roman and Johnson crossing Canal street. Lou has since moved to Prentiss street, which I hasten to add was changed from Calhoun in 1923 to bear its present name honoring Sergeant Prentiss, distinguished Mississippian. I wouldn't want Lou to move again; he bought this house.

After he left I examined page 180 more carefully, and the next two pages following. I discovered several other things that I wish I could push down into the swamp that all of the back-of-town once was. I had left out listing Marais among the streets that intersect Canal, and the historical importance of Marais in the nomenclature is revealed on page 67. When Marais crosses Canal it becomes LaSalle on the uptown side, and with devilish consistency I left LaSalle out too. But I did not err in calling Treme street North Liberty. The city changed it back to bear the name of Claude Treme in 1951. Since publication of this book the city has changed more than a dozen street names; among them, part of Saratoga to Loyola and part of Loyola to Saratoga, part of Almonester (still misspelled Almonaster) to Franklin, and Arcade Place has become Board of Trade Place. At this writing Dryades street, from Howard to Canal, is being widened. When this work is done it will be a one-way street toward Canal; then University Place (first block of Dryades off Canal) is sure to disappear.

Further out Canal, I'm sorry I didn't omit all mention of Scott street, for I said on page 182 that Scott and Pierce are named for U. S. presidents. Franklin Pierce defeated Winfield Scott for the presidency in the election of 1852. The general got about the same number of electoral votes as Dixiecrat Strom Thurmond got ninety-five years later. Scott was no more a U. S. president than Thurmond was. On page 117, I don't know how the name of John Hampson, first mayor of Carrollton, came out Hampton; and

I'm equally mystified how Bernard Marigny got to be ninety-three years old on page 91. He was born in 1785, and lived eighty-three years, which was still enough for quite a life.

Then there's the chapter, "All Aboard For Uptown". In it on page 145 I have given a man's name to the Widow Delachaise. The street she named for herself was Antonine, not Antoine. In 1850, Antonine Foucher Delachaise's faubourg was among several that were joined together to form the City of Jefferson, which was incorporated March 9, of that year.

I'm embarrassed about the City of Jefferson. But maybe a lot of historians are also. It has been consistently absent from accounts of New Orleans, seemingly living so quiet an incorporated existence for twenty years that most writers have overlooked it. Even its early official records are mislaid. The City of Jefferson's boundaries were from Toledano to Joseph street, and from the river back to Freret; included within it was an older incorporation called the Borough of Freeport, whose modest boundaries were from Toledano to Napoleon, and the river to St. Charles Avenue. Freeport was incorporated in 1846, and through oversight wasn't *un*incorporated until a week after it became part of the City of Jefferson, which must have made for some corporate confusion.

Perhaps it should be explained that in the middle of the nineteenth century in the U. S. the terms city, town, village and borough were used interchangeably. Horace Greeley has commented: "It takes three log houses to make a city in Kansas, but they begin calling it a city as soon as they have staked out the lots." Lafayette (the present Garden District) was incorporated as a city. in 1850

Lafayette had a population of 14,190. Carrollton changed its designation from town to city in 1859, although its population then was scarcely 2,000. Jefferson obviously got its idea of being a city from Lafayette; and just as obviously Carrollton had the legislature change it to a city to keep in step. Since 1914, however, Louisiana state law has stipulated that a community of 150 people can become a village; 1,000 may call themselves a town; and not until the nose count reaches 5,000 can a community be called city.

But let the record show that the ante-bellum "cities" of Lafayette, Jefferson, and Carrollton (along with the borough of Freeport) are now the uptown wards of the City of New Orleans.

I have never been content about the origin of Westwego, as related in Chapter Thirteen. In the Research for *Frenchmen, Desire, Good Children,* I was late getting to the investigation of this curious name. In order to maintain a production schedule, research into its origin was hurried, and it is never wise to hurry research. I had been told, with some authority, how the name originated with the refugees of the Cheniere Caminada hurricane of 1893, and I gave this account on pages 195–196. Since publication of the book, it has been pointed out by my friend and colleague, Columnist Pie Dufour, that this is a rather incredible story; hard to believe. I could only agree that it was. So I undertook another, and more thorough investigation into the origin of Westwego.

Dozens of people, citizens of Westwego and others long associated with the region were interviewed. Scores of books and documents were consulted. For a time I feared I was one generation late in ever learning the true origin of this Jefferson Parish community, a city with a population of 9,719 in 1958. Then, finally, the pieces fitted together; and *this* is how it was:

In 1827, the Louisiana legislature chartered the Barataria and Lafourche Canal Company to dig a forty foot canal, six feet deep from the river to Bayou Segnette; and from there by various lakes and bayous and other canals, provide a continuous navigable waterway to Berwick Bay —present-day Morgan City. One arpent of land was secured from Camille Zeringue for the canal from the river back to Bayou Segnette.

This was during the "Canal Era" in America, a twenty-year period ushered in by the Erie Canal in 1817. There were many other successful canals in the east, and the Barataria and Lafourche Canal was a far-sighted effort, which should have fared better than its history of disappointments and failures reveal. Nevertheless, it provided New Orleans with its first direct communication with Grand Isle and the Barataria country. Packet boats, running on regular schedules, maintained this communication until into the twentieth century on the Company Canal—as this waterway came to be called.

This was the beginning of settlement in the Westwego area, for workmen had to be stationed at the river end of the Company Canal to collect tolls and operate the locks into the river. It was the beginning of settlement there, but not the beginning of the name of Westwego. This came forty years later. Strangely, a railroad going *east* to Mobile and Chattanooga is what started it all.

In 1866, the *New Orleans, Mobile and Chattanooga* was one of several railroads newly chartered in the New Orleans neighborhood. Its promoters were all eastern capitalists, foremost among them was Oakes Ames, New England manufacturer and vice president of the *Union Pacific,* said to be the man mostly responsible for the success of this first transcontinental railroad. However, Ames was a "product of his times" in the matter of railroad financing. Promoters of railroads in those days arranged credits and sold stocks so that railroad construction was financed with other people's money, but to the promoters' profit. The *New Orleans, Mobile and Chattanooga* was financed in this fiscal fashion.

Neverthelsss, by 1870 this line was complete to Mobile, and it's part of the *L&N* system of the present day. It was at about this time that the promoters decided not to build on to Chattanooga, but to go to Texas instead. This made the *New Orleans, Mobile and Chattanooga* a railroad with two divisions in New Orleans; one on the east bank going to Mobile, and another on the west bank to go west to Texas.

According to the railroad company's agreement with the state, this western division would commence at the western boundary of the city and run to the western boundary of the state. The city had just annexed Jefferson City and other lands which brought its western boundary to Carrollton; so the railroad immediately purchased the Millaudon plantation across the river from Napoleon Avenue, and changed its name to Amesville. The plans were to build the railroad's terminus there, with docks, wharves, and facilities for a railroad ferry. Then, the engineers discovered the riverfront of Amesville was a caving bank, too unstable for the river terminus of a railroad. But three miles upstream, just beyond the Company Canal, a secure riverbank was found; here a terminus could be established, and it was still just across the river from the city.

So the great plans for Amesville ended. The Ames family bought it from the railroad, and operated it in absentee ownership as a plantation for many years, never with great success. In 1908, the Marrero Land and Improvement Company acquired it. Today, Amesville is part of Marrero; and doing very well, as is all of the West Bank. But Marrero's Ames Blvd. still serves to recall its earlier hopes for an industrial success, which Old Man River washed away.

In the spring of 1871, construction of the railroad westward began at the Company Canal. This is the first mention of the name of Westwego, and it grew out of a series of meetings of the railroad's board of directors in faraway New York. They had purchased a huge plantation, only to find it useless for terminus purposes. "*Where* will we go west with the railroad," was the exasperating question before the board. Then, when the recommendations came in from the engineers that the Company Canal site was suitable, it was with great relief that they voted, "Then, *west we go* from there!" According to Miss Eleanor M. Muller of Westwego in 1959: "My father—Captain August Muller—said all the old timers of Westwego were sure that the place was named by some 'big business men from out of town'."

Unfortunately, construction of the "Chattanooga Railroad", as it was called for years after in Westwego, got no further west than Bayou Goula when its financing collapsed. Even though this western division's name had been changed to the *New Orleans, Mobile and Texas Railroad,* it never reached Texas. In 1875, the *New Or-*

leans and Pacific acquired the line. At first this latter company had planned to build a railroad down from Baton Rouge on the east side of the river, and the city had granted to the *New Orleans and Pacific* permission to locate its passenger terminal on Canal and Claiborne. When suddenly it appeared on the west bank, the city by Ordinance No. 6938, in 1881, leased the railroad all the riverfront of Audubon Park for ninety-nine years for $500 a year, so that it could ferry its trains over from Westwego at this point. Also, the city made it legal for the *N. O. & P.* to build a track through the park to South Claiborne, and down that street to the depot at Canal. Further permission was given to build more tracks along the riverfront, and in Jackson Avenue to Claiborne. Nobody can say the city wasn't making things attractive for the *N. O. & P.* and its tracks.

Matters were complicated, however, when the *Texas and Pacific Railroad* acquired the *New Orleans and Pacific,* and all of the privileges the city had granted. The *T. & P.* extended its westbank line from Westwego down almost to Algiers, and a ferry was installed at Thalia street. The T. & P. planned another ferry at Westwego, with a railroad track through the park, and down Claiborne to a depot at Canal—as the city had originally permitted. But in 1884, the city revoked the ordinances authorizing this. There were lawsuits and litigations that were not settled until 1910. Of such were the things that happened, and almost happened, because of Westwego; and the railroad that was started at the Company Canal in 1871.

But how did Westwego the railroad terminus become

Westwego the town, on the lower side of the Company Canal? In 1892, Pablo Sala bought this tract, had it subdivided into 162 lots, and named it Salaville. However, few bought Mr. Sala's $40 lots until after the 1893 hurricane at Cheniere Caminada. After that disaster, rescue boats went down the Company Canal. Some refugees were brought back then; others followed, until within five years several hundred lived on many $40 lots bought in the new subdivision. These people from the cheniere knew the river end of the canal as Westwego, and Westwego they called the town. When it was incorporated January 18, 1919 the population was 1,583; and in his proclamation, Governor Pleasant fixed the name as the "Village of Westwego."

Like the many tales of the various canals on Canal street, for which that thoroughfare was supposedly named, the Westwego story is complicated by numerous legends concerning its origin. Besides the "west we go" story of the refugees of Cheniere Caminada (which, incidentally, is still widely believed), another story tells of the empty boxcars in the *T. & P.* yards being chalk-marked "west we go" for their return westward for more loads of grain. Still another tells of Paddy O'Rorke, conductor on the *T. & P.*'s local, that went from McDonoghville to New Roads. "West we go!" Paddy would yell, when the train pulled out for its westward run from Westwego. There are other stories; and all of them explain how the name gained its popularity until its official adoption in 1919. But the fact remains, G. W. R. Bayley wrote in *The Picayune* on October 12, 1873 that it was Westwego when they started building *New Orleans, Mobile and*

Chattanooga westward from the Company Canal in 1871 —and Mr. Bayley was the railroad's chief engineer.

It appears amply evident, therefore, that I myself have double-crossed readers of the first edition of *Frenchmen, Desire, Good Children* regarding Westwego's origin. I am hopeful that readers of this second edition will straighten them out.

Questions have been raised on several other points in the book, that perhaps require a few words of amplification. One of these is the origin of "neutral ground", a term peculiar to New Orleans for centers of divided streets. Probably the first explanation of neutral ground is by George Cable in 1884: * "The people of New Orleans take pride in Canal street. . . . Its two distinct granite paved roadways are each forty feet wide, and the tree-bordered 'neutral ground' measures fifty-four feet across. It was 'neutral' when it divided between the French Quarter and the Americans at the time when their municipality governments were distinct from each other." In 1896, the Louisiana Supreme Court gave judicial explanation to the term in rendering an opinion concerning the neutral ground of Carrollton Avenue. Said the court: "This expression 'neutral ground' has occasioned some confusion . . . (it) had its origin in the *unclaimed part* of Canal street. . . . It has no significance in its application to other streets."

But custom has overruled the court. Neutral ground has become the name for the middle of every divided street in New Orleans. From this beginning, it has also

---

* In the *Daily Crescent* of April 22, 1862, "the neutral ground on Canal street" is mentioned as though the term was already well known.

been heard in other cities referring to the centers of their divided streets.

Each Sunday, since observing its centennial in 1937, *The Times-Picayune* has reprinted selected 100-year-old items from the files of the old *Picayune*. It has been called to my attention that several things in this book are at variance with *The Way The Picayune Saw It*. This venerable old newspaper will get no argument from me; after all, the *Picayune* was *there*!

The street named for Peter Conrey, like those named for Almonester and Zimpel, is misspelled in the nomenclature. It is also misspelled in this book on pages 110 and 121. Files show that Margaret Abrams died March 4, 1848, not in 1857 as I say on page 126. (This is a typographical error; March 11, 1857 was the year Caldwell legally adopted Margaret's sons.) Philippa street, named for Carondelet's daughter, was actually called Philippa for some years after the founding of the university there in 1834. (I didn't know that—see page 71.) In 1849 the *Picayune* reported how a mysterious fire razed two buildings which hastened the opening of Commercial Alley. (I didn't know about this fire, but I was aware that shabby buildings standing in the way of progress had a curious way of burning down in those days.) Carroll street, I am told, was so called in the late 1850s. The heroic policeman (see page 214) wasn't even born then, so the street is obviously named for Gen. Carroll of Tennessee, for whom Carrollton appears to have been named. Also, there is some doubt that Canal street ever received its legacy from Judah Touro, little evidence that he left such a legacy, and a report that the legacy was taken away. That's frequently the way it is with wills . . . and all of this is the way the *Picayune* saw it. Thanks, *Picayune*!

There have been many inquiries about the origin of Colapissa street, since the opening of Earhart Blvd. to Carrollton Ave. Jutting out of that busy intersection, Colapissa is much more noticeable now. Origin of the name is just as explained on pages 232–33. However, new evidence indicates that there actually was a camp of these Indians in the vicinity when Zimpel was subdividing Carrollton.

Busy Earhart Boulevard was the first of the new expressways completed. It is named for Fred A. Earhart, who was Commissioner of Public Utilities in 1947, when the city and the railroads were negotiating the Union Station and grade separations program. The boulevard was built in 1952 along the former right-of-way of a railroad. In the Union Station vicinity, Earhart Boulevard is overshadowed by the elevated lanes of the Pontchartrain Expressway, the city's first limited access highway which was nearing completion in 1959. When finished, Pontchartrain Expressway will provide non-stop automobile passage from the north shore of Lake Pontchartrain, over the lake, through the city and over the river to the Westbank Expressway, and to U. S. 90 westbound.

If any one project of the last ten years can be reckoned head and shoulders above all others, it would have to be the Greater New Orleans Mississippi River Bridge, towering high as the Washington Monument for its 1,575 foot leap of the river. It's the world's largest cantilever type highway bridge. Its approaches double its length; and its 110 foot breadth amply accommodates four lanes of traffic and two pedestrian walks. In all the 15,000 navigable miles of the Mississippi and its tributaries no greater bridge crosses its watery way than this $65,000,-000 * structure of gleaming steel. Yet, superlative as are the bridge's statistics, its political record is no less remarkable. Orleanians have dreamed of a bridge in the city limits for nearly one hundred years, but not until 1948 when Captain Neville Levy began pushing for legislation to build pay-as-you-go bridges and tunnels were those dreams ever more than dreams—or politicians' promises. In 1952, Act. No. 7 of the legislature created the Mississippi River Bridge Authority; with Governor Robert Kennon's signature it became law on June 13. Six years later—April 15, 1958—first cars began rolling across the bridge. This same pay-as-you-go enabling legislation also made possible the Pontchartrain Causeway, which opened August 29, 1956. $46,000,000 in bonds were sold to finance the causeway, which is really a bridge over twenty-four miles of open water. Most of the length of the Pontchartrain Expressway through the city follows the right-of-way of the New Basin Canal, now all filled up. Funny thing; it cost $774,930 more to fill up the New Basin, than it cost to dig it in 1832.

The name of Captain Neville Levy, father of the river bridge and of pay-as-you-go authority which made such bridges into realities, will forever be identified with the Greater New Orleans Mississippi River Bridge, as his bridge has been officially titled. The year of its completion, Captain Levy was the recipient of every civic award the citizenry could think up, with the exception of No. 1

* Amount of bonds sold. In 1959 actual construction costs estimated as much as twenty per cent less.

Beaver of the Beaver Patrol. It hadn't been thought up yet.

Another name not soon forgotten will be deLesseps S. Morrison, mayor of the city during the years of all this activity. But Morrison Avenue, downtown in Gentilly, isn't named for him. His Honor wasn't even born in New Roads in 1910, when M. L. Morrison, Frank B. Haynes, Robert H. Downman, and others organized the New Orleans Lakeshore Land Company, and subdivided this area. The company met disaster in the hurricane of 1915. Morrison Avenue, Hayne Boulevard and Downman Road —familiar street names since World War II—are named for them. Other men prominent in the ill-fated enterprise, whose names are still identified with roads and canals in the region include Jahncke, Cannon, Dwyer, Benson, Berg, Lawrence and Lamb.

In retrospect, perhaps, the decade that has passed since publication of *Frenchmen, Desire, Good Children* may one day be pointed out as one of transition. Certainly the story I wrote, the story of the historic street nomenclature of the city, has been told. What follows belongs to the future, not in the past. It remains for another book at some future time to evaluate this decade, and to explain how it ushered in a much greater New Orleans—if indeed it did.

As for this book—for the most part a book of unforgettable names—it ends here. In 1949, Robert L. Crager & Company (Bob and Tess) first published it. In 1957 Bob's many friends were sorrowed to learn of his death in New York. In my book Bob Crager's is a name that shall not be forgotten either.

And this is my book.

INDEX

Index

Index

Index

Index

261

Index

Index

Index

Index

Index

INDEX

(For Chapter Sixteen)

Index